Praise for Sugarcane...

Arlyn has the rare gift among recipe writers of creating the most interesting, most unexpected, most delicious culinary ideas (mochi stuffed chocolate chip cookies! southeast tiramisu!!) while never losing sight of the need to keep techniques approachable for the home cook. This is a book you will want to—and be able to—cook from cover to cover.

—**Daniel Gritzer, Culinary Director,** *Serious Eats*

Sugarcane by Arlyn Osborne offers a delightful fusion of traditional Filipino desserts and a touch of American familiarity. Drawing inspiration from her childhood memories, Osborne presents a collection of enticing recipes that exude the rich flavors and vibrant spirit of Filipino cuisine. With clever twists and creative adaptations, she seamlessly combines the best of both worlds to create mouthwatering treats that will please both Filipino food enthusiasts and those eager to explore new taste sensations.

— **Leah Cohen, chef and owner of Pig & Khao and Piggyback NYC**

The imagery is captivating and the recipes are delicious. But this is more than a cookbook. Sugarcane is a fascinating glance into Philippine history, folklore, and tradition. Through intimate details and thoughtful reflection, it's a beautifully written coming of age story that brings to light the tension and texture of juggling two cultures and identities at once.

—**Jordan Andino, chef and owner of Flip Sigi & Carriage House NYC**

Sugarcane

Sugarcane

Sweet Recipes from
My Half-Filipino Kitchen

Hardie Grant

PUBLISHING

Arlyn Osborne

photographs by Linda Xiao

Hardie Grant

NORTH AMERICA

Hardie Grant North America
2912 Telegraph Ave
Berkeley, CA 94705
hardiegrantusa.com

Library of Congress Cataloging-in-Publication Data
is available upon request.

ISBN: 9781958417249
ISBN (eBook): 9781958417331
Printed in China

Design by Amanda Jane Jones
First Edition

FSC
www.fsc.org

MIX
Paper | Supporting
responsible forestry
FSC™ C020056

For my family, near and far.

Cakes

Cookies & Bars

Pies, Tarts & Crisps

Puddings, Custards & Jellies

Contents

Breads & Pastries

Frozen Sweets

Introduction

I took the C train downtown and got off at 14th Street. There had been delays, and as usual, I was running a little late. I checked my phone for directions and glanced around at the street signs. The black knife bag slung around my right shoulder felt like

It was the absence of food that fed my obsession with it.

sixty pounds, and it was thumping against my thigh with every forceful step. I shuffled hurriedly into Chelsea Market, contorting my body like a contemporary dancer through idle crowds and made my way to elevator 22. I'd taken a photo in front of it only three years ago, posing with one hand on my hip and the other pointing at the sign. This time, though, I was actually getting on. After finishing culinary school and a magazine internship, I was minutes away from a technical interview at Food Network. My heart was beating like a drum.

The test kitchen was loud and active, and my eyes couldn't keep up with where to look. Two large cameras drifted along the first workstation, and behind it, rows of people methodically slicing and stirring and sautéing. A thick wooden cutting board had been set

up for me, and on command, I produced an array of various cuts and fine dices while I managed to not chop my finger off. Instead of asking me about a time I showed leadership or went above and beyond, I was tasked with preparing a few dishes. Things were going fine until they weren't. Every negative thought invaded my mind. What if I messed it up? What if I actually didn't know what I was doing? What if I didn't belong here? Pots boiled, timers went off, people called out "behind" in stern, resolute voices. The sound of chaos was ready to swallow me. I could leave. I looked at the door. No one was forcing me to stay. But if I wanted to be there, I'd have to add to the noise. I cranked on my burner until it snapped like a whip, a halo of blue flames emerging with a steady hum. I whisked eggs to high froth. Minced herbs into mere slivers. And melted butter over low, controlled heat. Like it always had before, cooking helped me make sense of things.

It's never been easy to decide which version of myself to be. Or how to rightly be both.

My mother claims my sweet tooth is due to her sugarcane cravings when she was pregnant with me. I don't have another theory, so maybe she's right. Food was a large part of both my parents' upbringing. My mom, the middle of eleven children, grew up on a farm in Luzon, the largest island in the Philippines. Her family home, lush with tropical fruit and radiant flowers, stretches across acres, bordered by vibrant undulating rice fields and groves of sugarcane. My grandparents, whom I call Lolo and Lola, sold produce every day of the year at a local palengke, or wet market, in Paniqui. Before and after school, my mom and her siblings would prepare sweet coconut treats, called bukayo, for sale. My two oldest uncles would cook. My mom and her sisters would package. And the other brothers would peddle them on the streets and sell them wholesale to convenience stores, called sari-saris, where kids could buy a single

piece for a few pesos. My paternal grandfather worked as a baker in Devon, England, before moving his family to the States. He'd rise every morning before the sun, bake trays of hand-kneaded bread, and return home powdered in a veil of thin flour. Despite this, neither of my parents routinely cooked when I was growing up.

The truth is, food wasn't important to my parents. They considered cooking a chore. And anything remotely involved was reserved for special occasions. On most days, our meals came from the freezer aisle or fast-food chains, whatever was swift and simple. Our home was not overflowing with love. And like many Asian families, we never engaged in physical affection or vocalized it either.

Still, I was no stranger to the connection between food and love. I saw it. At my friends' houses, on TV, and even within my own extended family. When we traveled to the Philippines (which was only a couple of times), my Lolo and Lola, aunts and uncles, even my cousins, would work tirelessly preparing food. And it looked hard. They built fires, filled buckets of water from a pump, pried coconuts

from the tallest treetops, and spent countless hours rolling sweet and savory fillings inside emerald-green banana leaves and fawn-colored pastry wrappers. Stateside, Fil-Am potluck parties emitted a similar atmosphere. Buffet tables piled high with disposable aluminum pans, each brimming with saucy salty meats, tangled noodles, crispy fried fare, spears of mango, and sticky glutinous sweets. In those moments, food was at the fulcrum of our existence. I witnessed the happiness it conjured. The love it demonstrated. The power it had to bring people together. And I wanted it for myself. That's how I fell in love with cooking. It was the absence of food that fed my obsession with it. And somewhere along the way, it proffered a journey of self-discovery.

Growing up, the food at my family table fit neatly into one of two categories: Filipino or American. They coexisted but never coalesced. Much like my cultural identity. What it means to be Asian American today is a lot different than what it meant when I was growing up. I started school in Japan, where I was born, but the place I call home

Cooking is a way for me to speak when I cannot find the words to express myself, or, rather, bring myself to say the things I wish I could.

is a small sandy town in the Southern Outer Banks of North Carolina. Living in an isolated, primarily white society meant my exposure to an Asian-American community was scarce. I wasn't the only Asian student in my school (though I was in my grade); there were a couple others. But we didn't rally together, confirm similarities, or bond over it. I think we were all just focused on blending in and protecting ourselves from hurtful stereotypes. At least, I know I was. Being Asian was like keeping a small secret to myself. I avoided certain conversations just like I avoided bringing Asian food to the cafeteria because I didn't want to advertise my otherness. Yet, even in the company of my Filipino family, I still felt different. To them, I'm mestiza, which means "mixed," with lighter skin and the inability to converse in native Tagalog, putting more than geographical distance between me and many of my relatives. Being half Asian might theoretically present only half the struggles. But in my experience, it created double the confusion. It's never been easy to decide which version of myself to be. Or how to rightly be both.

Perhaps more than anything, cooking has helped me find myself. It's allowed me to make sense of who I am. This collection of recipes is a personal story told through food, illustrating what it means to me to be Filipino American. Some recipes are modified versions of classic dishes, like the Ube Coconut Cake (page 32) I make for my birthday, and the Maple Spam Shakoy (page 167) I make when I'm craving salty-sweet doughnuts, and the Buttermilk Berry Bibingka (page 46) I like to whip up on weekend afternoons. Other recipes here are designed by my Asian-American pantry, like the Chili Crisp Chocolate Chunk Cookies

(page 63) that are kissed with MSG, and the Kumquat Curd Bars (page 60) that taste like the tropical sun, and the Lemongrass Vanilla Scones (page 171) that are deliciously fragrant.

When I first took up cooking, there was no clear objective in mind. It was a lifeline. And I just ran with it. When I left Chelsea Market that chilly October day, I felt a sense of belonging I hadn't felt before. Cooking helped me find community. I spent four years at Food Network before forging ahead as a contributor for brands like Serious Eats, Food52, Delish, *The Washington Post*, and *Bon Appétit*. I've met talented writers and gifted chefs who have coached me, believed in me, given me the space to share my story, and opened my eyes to new ones. I find comfort in formulating steps, knowing that if I follow them I'll create something whole and beautiful from nothing. Cooking is a way for me to speak when I cannot find the words to express myself, or, rather, bring myself to say the things I wish I could. *I love you*, and *I'm sorry*, and *congratulations*. *I'm glad we're friends*. Cooking has given me a sense of self and direction. It's allowed me to preserve the past and build my future. It's helped me see myself, to be myself. It's given me the capacity to dream. ●

A Short Note on Ingredients

I'm not going to regale you with what's in my pantry or wordy definitions about every ingredient in this book (I'm pretty sure you know how to use Google). But there are a few items I really must call out.

Canned Unsweetened Coconut Milk Canned coconut milk is a wildly inconsistent product. Texture, viscosity, and taste vary by brand. All my recipes have been developed with A Taste of Thai unsweetened coconut milk—the regular, full-fat version (not the lite version). This is my go-to. It's not too thick, not too thin, and available at most supermarkets and online. My second choice is Chaokoh.

Freeze-Dried Mango If you want to make the Mango Coconut Rolls (page 156)—and I promise you do—the brand of freeze-dried mango is everything. I tested with multiple brands. Nothing compares to Great Value from Walmart or Crispy Fruit from Crispy Green.

Ube Paste, Pandan Paste, etc. I use the ube paste from Butterfly. This brand carries a lot of great flavors, like pandan, lychee, and jackfruit—which I also use. You can find it in Asian supermarkets and online.

Glutinous Rice Flour and Rice Flour These aren't the same thing. Glutinous rice flour (also called "sweet rice flour") is made from sticky rice and produces a chewy consistency. For glutinous rice flour, I recommend mochiko from the brand Koda Farms or the brand Erawan. For rice flour, I like Erawan or Bob's Red Mill.

Chocolate Bars My go-to chocolate is one with 70% cacao (classified as bittersweet).

I'm also Team Chopped Chocolate. Chocolate chips often have stabilizers in them, which means they don't melt so well. And aesthetically speaking, I just don't like how they look when they're baked into cookies. Chopped chocolate will create gooey, melty puddles in your cookies, which taste and look better.

Cocoa Powder My recipes call for unsweetened cocoa powder that has been Dutch-processed (or "Dutched"), meaning it's been treated to neutralize its acidity (this effectively gives it a darker color and more chocolatey flavor).

Natural cocoa powder (because of its higher acidity) is often used in recipes that rely on baking soda, whereas Dutch process cocoa powder generally teams up with baking powder (and, sometimes, a little bit of baking soda).

Unsweetened Shredded Coconut and Flakes I always use unsweetened shredded coconut, so I can control the sugar myself. I consider shredded coconut to be those tiny, slivered pieces. Some brands do call this size "shredded." Others use "flakes."

I occasionally call for coconut flakes, which I consider to be those larger, shaved pieces. Some brands call this size "flakes." Others use "chips." It's annoying, but I hope this clears things up.

Ube Halaya This Philippine purple yam jam is a pantry staple for me, which means you'll see it quite a bit in this book. This product can be found in Asian supermarkets and online.

Kosher Salt Diamond Crystal kosher salt is the standard choice within the culinary industry. Nothing else sprinkles quite like it. If you can't find it in stores, know that it's readily available online.

Keep in mind that not all kosher salt measures and weighs the same. For example: 1 teaspoon of Diamond Crystal kosher salt weighs 3 g, whereas 1 teaspoon of Morton Kosher salt weighs 5 g, and 1 teaspoon of table salt weighs 7 g. ●

An Even Shorter Section on Equipment

Oven Thermometer I think this is probably the most vital piece of culinary equipment. Just because you set your oven to 350°F (180°C) doesn't mean it's actually calibrated correctly. Most ovens aren't. When someone claims a recipe took much longer to bake, oven temperature (unknowingly) is usually the culprit. I like the kind with a probe so I can also use it for frying.

→ **Note:** All of my bakes take place on the center rack of the oven unless otherwise specified.

Kitchen Scale I consider this the second-most-important piece of equipment. If you read "A Case for Weighing" (page 12), then you know how I feel. I recommend the brands Ozeri and Escali.

Sheet Pans If you've ever made cookies or biscuits that bake perfectly except the bottoms are burned, then you're probably not using quality sheet pans (assuming the oven temperature isn't to blame).

The quality of your sheet pans matters. Thin, flimsy aluminum sheet pans aren't going to distribute the heat as well as thick, sturdy ones. You can't go wrong with Nordic Ware. But if the bargain stuff is all you've got, try doubling up your pans.

Square and Rectangular Baking Pans I prefer pans that have straight sides (not angled) and sharp edges (not rounded). It's all very clean looking, and parchment paper fits seamlessly in all the corners. Ateco and Magic Line have great options. When it comes to loaf pans, I reach for ones with straighter sides (but I'm not too picky about the edges).

Note: If a recipe calls for a baking pan, that means it's aluminum. A baking dish, on the other hand, indicates glass or ceramic.

Stand Mixer and Electric Hand Mixer I call for these appliances a lot in my recipes and use the KitchenAid brand for both. The chart shows how I navigate the speed settings. If you're using a different brand, adjust accordingly.

Stand Mixer	Electric Hand Mixer
Stir = lowest	1 = low
2 = low	2 = medium-low
4 = medium-low	3 = medium
6 = medium	4 = medium-high
8 = medium-high	5 = high
10 = high	

Small Food Processor Do what you like, but I prefer using a small food processor for smaller jobs. KitchenAid and Cuisinart make mini versions. But I just use my immersion blender with the chopping bowl carafe (I have the one by Breville).

Pots and Pans Pans and skillets are measured by their overall diameter (the top)—*not* the cooking surface diameter (the bottom). For example, a 10-inch skillet will measure 10 inches (25 cm) across the top. But the diameter of its cooking surface will measure around 8 inches (20 cm).

Sizing (i.e., small, medium, large) can be very subjective. Below is my interpretation.

Small skillet = 8 inches (20 cm)
Medium skillet = 10 inches (25 cm)
Large skillet: 12 inches (30 cm)
Small saucepan/saucier =
    1 to 1½ quarts (1 to 1.5 L)
Medium saucepan/saucier =
    2 to 3 quarts (2 to 3 L)
Large saucepan/saucier =
    3½ to 4 quarts (3.5 to 4 L)
Dutch oven (for frying) =
    4 quarts (4 L) and up

Note: A saucepan has straight sides. A saucier has rounded sides (making it better suited for things that constantly need whisking or stirring). I use the term *saucepan* in my recipes, since it's more universal. I personally prefer a saucier. But both will get the job done.

Measuring Tape I'm referring to the ones you might see at the tailors to take body measurements. This is one of my favorite tools for cooking and baking. It's great for measuring anything.

A Warm Place When letting my yeast doughs rise, I like my "warm place" to be about 85°F (29°C). Sometimes I use my oven with a digital probe thermometer. Sometimes it's my pantry with a space heater. Sometimes I find a shady spot outside on a hot summer day. How fast your dough rises will depend on your warm place. ●

Visual Cues

When I was in culinary school, my chef instructor slid an apple tart into the oven and clapped his hands. "How long does it bake?" I asked. He looked at me and with an arrogant smirk replied, "Until it's done."

This might be the most important lesson in cooking. The food will always tell you when it's ready. You just have to look. This is why you must pay attention to the visual cues: thick like pudding, reduced to ½ cup, stiff peaks, golden brown, a toothpick comes out clean, etc.

The cook times I provide are guidelines. Pretty good ones, I'd add. But you can't always take my word for it. Even when you've done all you can to eliminate major margins of error—you've used a scale to measure your ingredients and you have an oven thermometer to gauge the correct temperature—there are still plenty of variables that are subject to interpretation. What does the flame of medium-high heat look like? Or the rate of bubbling during a simmer? There are also elements that are outside of your control entirely. Like the weather: the temperature and humidity.

So, please, keep an eye on things. Follow the estimated timings. But also watch for the visual cues. ●

A Case for Weighing

If I asked ten people to measure out 1 cup of flour, I'd probably get ten different amounts of flour. This is why I prefer to cook using weight rather than volume.

Even still, there isn't a standardized universal conversion table. How one person converts 1 cup of volume to weight is still subject to interpretation.

The following chart (page 18) can act as your guide as you cook through this book (and beyond, if you'd like).

All my recipes include weight measurements as well as corresponding volumes where possible.

Random Reasons to Love Weight More Than Volume (Aside from Consistency)

● Fewer dishes to clean (i.e., measuring cups)
● When you divide batters or doughs, you can weigh the entire amount first and calculate how much each portion should be.
● Some things (like kumquats) are just plain fiddly to measure by volume.

→ See conversion chart on page 18.

Conversion Chart

ingredient	1 cup	¾ cup	⅔ cup	½ cup	⅓ cup	¼ cup	1 Tbsp	1 tsp
flours + starches + grains								
all-purpose flour bread flour glutinous rice flour	125 g	94 g	83 g	62 g	41 g	31 g	8 g	2.5 g
cake flour coconut flour rice flour	110 g	82 g	73 g	55 g	36 g	27 g	7 g	2 g
almond flour	80 g	60 g	53 g	40 g	26 g	20 g	5 g	1.5 g
arrowroot flour cornstarch	132 g	99 g	88 g	66 g	44 g	33 g	8 g	2.5 g
cashew flour	103 g	78 g	70 g	52 g	35 g	26 g	7 g	2 g
small pearl tapioca	190 g	144 g	126 g	95 g	63 g	48 g	12 g	4 g
boba pearls	160 g	120 g	106 g	80 g	53 g	40 g	10 g	3 g
sticky rice	200 g	150 g	133 g	100 g	66 g	50 g	12 g	4 g
old-fashioned oats	100 g	75 g	66 g	50 g	33 g	25 g	6 g	2 g
sweeteners								
granulated sugar light brown sugar dark brown sugar	200 g	150 g	133 g	100 g	66 g	50 g	12 g	4 g
powdered sugar	100 g	75 g	66 g	50 g	33 g	25 g	6 g	2 g
maple syrup (pure) agave nectar light corn syrup dark corn syrup golden syrup	300 g	225 g	200 g	150 g	100 g	75 g	19 g	6 g
honey molasses	350 g	262 g	233 g	175 g	117 g	88 g	22 g	7 g
sweetened condensed milk	300 g	225 g	200 g	150 g	100 g	75 g	19 g	6 g

ingredient	1 cup	¾ cup	⅔ cup	½ cup	⅓ cup	¼ cup	1 Tbsp	1 tsp
spreads								
ube halaya natural peanut butter	248 g	186 g	166 g	124 g	83 g	62 g	15 g	5 g
nutella	280 g	210 g	187 g	140 g	93 g	70 g	18 g	6 g
sesame paste	240 g	180 g	160 g	120 g	80 g	60 g	15 g	5 g
jam	320 g	240 g	213 g	160 g	107 g	80 g	20 g	6.5 g
miscellaneous								
milk powder	80 g	60 g	53 g	40 g	27 g	20 g	5 g	1.5 g
malted milk powder	110 g	82 g	73 g	55 g	36 g	27 g	7 g	2 g
cocoa posder graham cracker crumbs	100 g	75 g	66 g	50 g	33 g	25 g	6 g	2 g
diamond crystal kosher salt	140 g	105 g	93.3 g	70 g	46.6 g	35 g	9 g	3 g
unsweetened shredded coconut	50 g	37 g	32 g	25 g	16 g	12 g	3 g	1 g
seeds + nuts								
sesame seeds pecans (whole) cashews (whole) almonds (whole)	140 g	105 g	93 g	70 g	47 g	35 g	9 g	3 g
fats + oils								
neutral oil coconut oil	210 g	156 g	140 g	105 g	70 g	52 g	13 g	4 g
butter	226 g 2 sticks	170 g 1½ sticks	150 g	113 g 1 stick	75 g	56 g 4 Tbsp	14 g 1 Tbsp	5 g
liquids								
water coconut water whole milk heavy cream buttermilk canned coconut milk fruit juice liquid extracts vanilla bean paste	240 g	180 g	160 g	120 g	80 g	60 g	15 g	5 g
evaporated milk	250 g	186 g	166 g	125 g	83 g	62 g	16 g	5 g

01

Cakes

Maja Blanca Custard Cake

Corn and coconut are a beloved duo in both sweet and savory cooking across Southeast Asia. It's a classic combination that harmonizes much like peanut butter and jelly. But softer, gentler. More nuanced. An unassuming perpetual crowd-pleaser.

This recipe transforms Filipino maja blanca, a corn-studded coconut gelatin, into a luscious custard-covered cake. Creamy corn puree adds a warm buttery tone and extra moisture to the fluffy cake. The thick blanket of ivory coconut pudding on top is silky and supple but stable enough to cut neatly into squares. A hint of lemon pierces through the richness, while a pile of toasted coconut lends a nutty crunch to every mouthful.

For the sweet corn cake: Preheat the oven to 350°F (180°C). Grease a 9-inch (23 cm) square cake pan with cooking spray and line the bottom with parchment paper.

In a small food processor, add the corn and puree until creamy but still a little chunky. Transfer to a large bowl and whisk in the eggs, oil, sugar, lemon juice, and salt. Whisk in the flour and baking powder until just combined.

Scrape the batter into the prepared pan and smooth into an even layer. Bake until the top is dry and a toothpick inserted into the center of the cake comes out clean, about 25 minutes. Transfer the pan to a wire rack and let cool completely.

For the coconut pudding: In a large saucepan, whisk together the coconut milk, sugar, cornstarch, and salt. Cook over medium-high heat, whisking constantly, until thick like pudding, about 5 minutes.

Transfer the pudding to a medium bowl, and whisk in the lemon juice and coconut extract. Cover with plastic wrap so it touches the surface of the pudding directly (this will prevent a skin from forming). Let cool at room temperature for 30 minutes (it should still be a little warm).

To assemble: Spread the coconut pudding over the cake and top with the toasted coconut. Cover with foil and refrigerate until firm, at least 3 hours. ●

MAKES ONE 9-INCH (23 CM) SQUARE CAKE

Sweet Corn Cake and Garnish

One 11 oz. (312 g) can corn kernels, drained

2 large eggs, at room temperature

¾ cup (156 g) neutral oil

½ cup (100 g) granulated sugar

1 tablespoon (15 g) fresh lemon juice

½ teaspoon kosher salt

1¼ cups (156 g) all-purpose flour

1 teaspoon baking powder

Coconut Pudding:

Two 13.5 fl. oz. (400 ml) cans unsweetened coconut milk

1 cup (200 g) granulated sugar

½ cup (66 g) cornstarch

¼ teaspoon kosher salt

1 tablespoon (15 g) fresh lemon juice

2 teaspoons coconut extract

1 cup (50 g) unsweetened shredded coconut, toasted

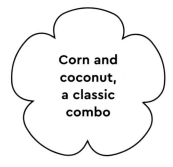

Corn and coconut, a classic combo

Cakes

Sugarcane

Raspberry Buko Pandan Cake

In Southeast Asia, pandan cake might be as generic as vanilla cake in the States. Each country has its own variation, and in the Philippines, instead of being served plain, it's always adorned with cream and coconut strips—either buko (young coconut meat from standard coconut trees) or macapuno (coconut meat from dwarf mutant coconut trees). Both have a soft, jelly-like texture. And although buko can be sourced fresh or frozen, macapuno is often purchased in preserved, jarred form.

The cake, a chiffon, is bouncy and delicate and painted an herbal shade of green, courtesy of the pandan, whose rich natural pigments are as pronounced as its flavor. This tropical shrub tastes like sweet grassy vanilla, with nutty and floral undertones.

A blanket of macapuno is hidden between the layers along with tangy raspberries, which also crown the upper tier like ruby gemstones. I love how the acidity interrupts the earthiness of the pandan, injecting a sudden burst of contrast in between bites—almost like you're diving into a cold pool on a hot day. Decorative peaks and swirls of whipped cream garnish the cake, forging a dessert that's as airy and weightless as a delicious cloud.

For the pandan cake: Preheat the oven to 350°F (180°C).

In a small food processor, add the pandan leaves and water and puree. Scrape down the sides as needed, and resist the urge to add more water. It won't look like it's blending well, but you just want to get the pandan really pulverized.

Place a fine-mesh sieve over a liquid measuring cup and strain the mixture, pressing with a rubber spatula to extract the green liquid (discard the solids). You should have 1/3 cup (80 g) pandan juice (if you're short for whatever reason, add a little water). Set aside.

In a large bowl, add the egg yolks and 1/4 cup (50 g) sugar. Whisk by hand until thick and pale. Whisk in the pandan juice, oil, and salt. Sift in the cake flour and baking powder and whisk until just combined.

To the bowl of a stand mixer fitted with the whisk, add the egg whites and cream of tartar. Beat on medium speed until foamy, about 1 minute. Increase the speed to medium-high and slowly add 1/2 cup (100 g) of the sugar (it takes about 1 minute to add all the sugar). Continue beating until stiff peaks form (peaks should stand straight up and not curl at the tip), 3 to 5 minutes.

Fold the meringue into the pandan mixture in three additions.

Scrape the batter into an 8-inch (20 cm) aluminum chiffon cake pan with a removable bottom. Bake until the top is light golden and a toothpick inserted into the center of the cake comes out clean, about 30 minutes.

Transfer the pan to a wire rack and let cool for 10 minutes. Run a small offset spatula around the perimeter to loosen the edges. Using the removable bottom, separate the cake from the pan. Place the cake (right side up) on a wire rack and let cool completely. Slice the cake in half horizontally to create two layers.

(Recipe continued on following page).

MAKES ONE 8-INCH (20 CM) TWO-LAYER CAKE

Pandan Cake

10 frozen pandan leaves, cut into small pieces (about 80 g) (see Note)

1/3 cup (80 g) water

4 large eggs, separated, at room temperature

3/4 cup (150 g) granulated sugar, divided

1/4 cup (52 g) neutral oil

1/2 teaspoon kosher salt

1 cup (110 g) cake flour

1 1/2 teaspoons baking powder

1/4 teaspoon cream of tartar

Filling and Garnish

3 tablespoons (45 g) cold tap water

2 teaspoons (6 g) unflavored gelatin powder

2 1/2 cups plus 2 teaspoons (610 g) heavy cream, cold, divided

1/4 cup (50 g) granulated sugar

1/3 cup (93 g) jarred macapuno, rinsed, drained, and dried well

6 oz. (170 g) fresh raspberries

Special Equipment

8-inch (20 cm) aluminum chiffon cake pan with removable bottom (see Note)

Notes: The removable bottom eliminates the need for cooking spray. This allows the batter to climb (grab onto the sides) as it rises, creating a tall and lofty cake.

To use two 8-inch (20 cm) aluminum cake pans, line the bottom with parchment paper but don't grease the sides.

In place of frozen pandan leaves, combine the 1/3 cup (80 g) water with 1/8 teaspoon green pandan paste.

24

(Raspberry Buko Pandan Cake continued from previous page).

For the filling: In a small bowl, add the water and sprinkle the gelatin evenly over top. Whisk together and let absorb for 5 minutes. Microwave until melted, 5 to 10 seconds. Whisk in 2 teaspoons (10 g) of the heavy cream.

In the bowl of a stand mixer fitted with the whisk, beat the remaining 2 ½ cups (600 g) of heavy cream and sugar on medium speed until it starts to thicken, about 1 minute. With the mixer on the lowest speed, gradually pour in the gelatin. Increase to medium speed and beat until fluffy but firm, about 1 minute.

To assemble: Place the bottom cake layer (cut side up) on a cake plate. Top with 1 cup of whipped cream and spread evenly.

Transfer the remaining whipped cream to a piping bag fitted with a large star tip (such as Wilton 8B). Pipe dollops of the cream around the perimeter of the cake to make a border. Scatter the macapuno in the center of the cake, inside the piped border. Top with ½ cup (70 g) of the raspberries. Place the second cake layer on top (cut side down).

Using the remaining whipped cream, pipe a decorative even layer over the top of the cake. Then, pipe dollops around the perimeter to make a border. Dot the remaining raspberries around the perimeter (one berry per dollop) to create a border. ●

Strawberry Mango Pianono

Pianono, the Filipino equivalent of a Swiss roll, is traditionally filled with sweetened margarine. The cake is typically a chiffon, which relies on beaten egg whites to create an airy texture and a soft chew. Instead, my version opts for a simpler sponge: Whole eggs and sugar are whipped until pale and voluminous, creating a more tender crumb with less elasticity. Lofty mango cream and a ribbon of strawberry jam are tucked inside, revealing a marvelous swirl at every slice. It's airy, juicy, and bright. That's the simple beauty of a fruit and cream cake.

MAKES ONE 15-INCH (38 CM) JELLY ROLL

Cake

4 large eggs, at room temperature

½ cup (100 g) granulated sugar

⅛ teaspoon kosher salt

½ teaspoon vanilla extract

¾ cup (94 g) all-purpose flour

¾ teaspoon baking powder

Powdered sugar, for dusting

Filling and Topping

One 1 oz. (28 g) package freeze-dried mango (see Note)

1¾ cups (420 g) heavy cream, cold

¼ cup (50 g) granulated sugar

Pinch of kosher salt

6 tablespoons (120 g) strawberry jam

Diced Ataulfo yellow mango, for garnish

Thinly sliced strawberries, for garnish

Special Equipment

10½ × 15½-inch (27 × 39 cm) jelly roll pan

Note: Freeze-dried mango by Great Value or Crispy Fruit yields the best results.

For the cake: Preheat the oven to 400°F (200°C). Grease a 10½ × 15½-inch (27 cm × 39 cm) jelly roll pan with cooking spray and line the bottom with parchment paper.

To the bowl of a stand mixer fitted with the whisk, add eggs, granulated sugar, and salt. Beat on medium-high speed until thick, pale, and ribbony, 5 to 7 minutes. Beat in the vanilla.

Sift in the flour and baking powder and fold until just combined.

Scrape the batter into the prepared pan and spread into an even layer. Bake until golden and a toothpick inserted into the center of the cake comes out clean, about 10 minutes.

Meanwhile, place a clean tea towel on your work surface and sift a generous dusting of powdered sugar all over it.

Once the cake is finished baking, swiftly invert the pan onto the prepared tea towel and carefully remove the parchment. Fold about 3 inches (7.5 cm) of the tea towel over one of the short sides and position the cake so this side is closest to you. Tightly, but gently, roll the cake (with the tea towel tucked inside) away from you. Let cool completely, about 40 minutes.

For the filling: Using a spice grinder, grind the freeze-dried mango into a fine powder.

In the bowl of a stand mixer fitted with the whisk, beat the heavy cream, granulated sugar, and salt on medium speed until soft and sturdy peaks form, about 2 minutes. Transfer 1 cup (100 g) to a small bowl and set aside in the refrigerator (this is for the garnish).

Add the mango powder to the rest of the whipped cream in the stand mixer bowl and continue to beat on medium speed until stiff peaks form, about 30 seconds (it should have a little bit of a frosting look to it).

To assemble: Gently unroll the sponge. Gradually roll it back up (without the towel this time) and use a small paring knife to scrape off the visible golden "crust" from the exterior of the cake (it should peel right off, creating a flawless finish).

Unroll the sponge onto a sheet of parchment paper. Top with the jam and spread evenly. Top with the mango cream and spread evenly.

Starting with the same short side you started with before, roll up the cake. Using a serrated knife, slice a bit off from both ends.

Swiftly transfer the cake to a serving platter. Dollop the reserved whipped cream along the top of the cake and spread, swooping and swirling, to create soft whimsical peaks. Garnish with diced mangoes and sliced strawberries. ●

Chocolate Sesame Oil Cake

Throughout the writing of this book, my husband, Miles, has been very concerned with the number of chocolate offerings (he worships chocolate). Don't get me wrong. I like chocolate, too. Earthy and comforting, I find it's a natural match for a pantry staple of mine: sesame oil. I love this ingredient for its deeply nutty flavor, profound fragrance, and ability to add instant dimension. And while I use it mostly (basically, always) for savory cooking, these qualities are exactly what makes this cake so good.

This cake is moist and tender, covered with a thick chocolate and sesame paste ganache, and speckled with toasted sesame seeds for a bit of savory crunch. The ganache will set over time, but I like it best when it's still gooey, glossy, and warm.

For the sesame oil cake: Preheat the oven to 350°F (180°C). Grease a 9-inch (23 cm) round cake pan with cooking spray and line the bottom with parchment paper.

In a medium bowl, sift together the flour, cocoa powder, and baking powder.

In a liquid measuring cup, whisk together the boiling water and instant coffee.

To the bowl of a stand mixer fitted with the whisk, add the eggs, egg yolk, sugar, sesame oil, vanilla, and salt. Beat on medium-high speed until thickened and lightened in color, about 2 minutes. Beat in the sesame paste.

With the mixer on lowest speed, add half of the flour mixture and (immediately) half of the coffee mixture. Mix until just combined. Repeat, mixing until just combined.

Scrape the batter into the prepared cake pan. Bake until the top is dry and a toothpick inserted into the center of the cake comes out mostly clean with a few sticky crumbs, 32 to 34 minutes.

Transfer the pan to a wire rack and let cool for 10 minutes. Run a small offset spatula around the perimeter to loosen the edges. Invert the cake onto the wire rack. Remove the parchment. Invert again onto another wire rack so it sits right side up. Let cool completely before transferring to a cake plate.

For the sesame ganache and garnish: In a medium bowl, add the chocolate.

In a small saucepan, whisk together the heavy cream, sugar, sesame paste, and salt. Heat over medium heat until it just starts to simmer. Don't let it boil.

Pour the warm cream over the chocolate and let sit for 5 minutes. Whisk in the vanilla. Let the ganache cool for a minute or so. (Basically, you don't want the ganache to be too liquidy before pouring it over the cake. It should drip off the whisk thick and slow).

Pour the ganache over the cake, right in the center. Spread evenly, coaxing a few thick lazy drips over the sides in a few places. Let gravity do most of the work here. Sprinkle with the toasted sesame seeds. ●

MAKES ONE 9-INCH (23 CM) CAKE

Sesame Oil Cake

1 cup (125 g) all-purpose flour

½ cup (50 g) unsweetened Dutch process cocoa powder

1½ teaspoons baking powder

½ cup (120 g) boiling water

1½ teaspoons instant coffee or espresso powder

2 large eggs, at room temperature

1 large egg yolk, at room temperature

1 cup (200 g) granulated sugar

One 5 oz. (148 mL) bottle pure sesame oil (about ⅔ cup)

2 teaspoons vanilla extract

½ teaspoon kosher salt

2 tablespoons (30 g) sesame paste

Ganache and Garnish

2 oz. (56 g) dark chocolate (70% cacao), finely chopped

¼ cup (60 g) heavy cream

1 tablespoon (12 g) granulated sugar

1½ teaspoons (7 g) sesame paste

Pinch of kosher salt

¼ teaspoon vanilla extract

2 teaspoons black and white sesame seeds, toasted

Honey Salabat Tea Cake

When my mom was growing up, her family would listen to Boy Bautista on the local radio station each morning as he delivered the latest news to the province of Tarlac. He was charismatic, clear, and charming. The secret to his smooth confident voice, everyone knew, was a daily cup of salabat, a Filipino tea made with water and fresh ginger. This spicy elixir is warm and peppery and tickles the nose with every sip. Salabat is known to rejuvenate one's vocal cords, calm the nerves, and treat myriad illnesses. The lineage of ginger's healing powers can be traced back thousands of years to ancient China, and it is still a source of traditional medicine throughout the East.

Whenever my mom boiled a pot of salabat growing up, I'd add lots of lemon and honey, so it was sweet and tart and gingery. That's what this loaf cake tastes like. The flavor is almost medicinal—in a good way. A strong mug of amber salabat is stirred into the batter, baked, and topped with a sticky honey glaze and bits of chewy candied ginger. Every slice is sharp but soothing. I can't promise any health miracles or a career in voice-over, but I know after eating this cake, you'll definitely feel better.

For the salabat cake: Preheat the oven to 350°F (180°C). Grease a 9 × 5-inch (23 × 13 cm) loaf pan with cooking spray and line with parchment paper so there is overhang on both the long sides.

In a small saucepan, add the water and ginger and bring to a boil over high heat. Reduce to a very gentle simmer and cook, letting the flavors infuse, for 5 minutes. Turn off the heat, cover with a lid, and let steep for 10 minutes.

Place a fine-mesh sieve over a small liquid measuring cup and strain the mixture, pressing with a rubber spatula to extract the salabat. You should have ½ cup (120 g). If you have less, add a bit of water. Let cool for 10 minutes.

In a medium bowl, whisk together the flour, ground ginger, salt, baking powder, and baking soda.

In a large bowl, whisk together the cooled salabat, honey, oil, sugar, sour cream, eggs, lemon zest, lemon juice, and vanilla. Add the flour mixture all at once and whisk until just combined. The batter will be loose and lumpy like pancake batter.

Scrape the batter into the prepared loaf pan. Bake until golden and a wooden skewer inserted into the center of the cake comes out clean, about 1 hour. (Cover loosely with foil for the last 10 minutes to prevent overbrowning).

Transfer the pan to a wire rack set inside a foil-lined sheet pan (this will catch the glaze later) and let cool for 20 minutes. Using the parchment overhang as handles, lift the cake onto the wire rack. Discard the parchment and let the cake cool completely.

For the honey lemon glaze: In a small bowl, whisk together the powdered sugar, honey, lemon juice, and water. Drizzle the glaze down the center of the cooled cake and spread outward, letting gravity pull long drips down the sides. Top with the candied ginger. Let the glaze set before slicing and serving. ●

MAKES ONE 9 × 5-INCH (23 × 13 CM) LOAF CAKE

Salabat Cake

¾ cup (180 g) water

½ cup (80 g) diced peeled fresh ginger

1¾ cups (219 g) all-purpose flour

2 tablespoons (8 g) ground ginger

1 teaspoon kosher salt

½ teaspoon baking powder

½ teaspoon baking soda

½ cup (175 g) honey

½ cup (105 g) neutral oil

½ cup (100 g) granulated sugar

¼ cup (60 g) sour cream

2 large eggs, at room temperature

Grated zest of 1 large lemon

1 tablespoon (15 g) fresh lemon juice

1 teaspoon vanilla extract

Honey Lemon Glaze and Garnish

1 cup (100 g) powdered sugar

1 tablespoon (22 g) honey

2 teaspoons (10 g) fresh lemon juice

1 teaspoon (5 g) water

2 tablespoons (20 g) finely chopped crystallized ginger, for garnish

Ube Coconut Cake

Ube cakes are the crown jewel of Filipino cakes. They're traditionally made with spongy chiffon, known for its light and bouncy crumb. But my version, inspired by the many coconut cakes I enjoyed growing up in the American South, is tender and velvety. The layers are made with buttermilk and oil, which impart richness and moisture, and ube halaya (a Philippine yam jam), which lends a nutty vanilla flavor and a whimsical iris hue. The frosting (or icing, as they say in the South) is nothing more than sour cream, shredded coconut, and a little sugar. But it's tangy, fresh, and full of sumptuous shreds. And it's the version of coconut frosting I like best. Once the cake is assembled, it gets wrapped in plastic and refrigerated overnight. This gives the dried coconut time to rehydrate and allows excess moisture from the frosting to soak into the cake. This dessert unites two of my sweet obsessions—ube and coconut. In fact, it's so special, I make it for my birthday every year.

For the ube cake: Preheat the oven to 350°F (180°C). Grease two 9-inch (23 cm) round cake pans with cooking spray and line the bottoms with parchment paper.

In a medium bowl, whisk together the flour, baking powder, salt, and baking soda.

To the bowl of a stand mixer fitted with the whisk, add the ube halaya and beat until smooth. Add the sugar and beat on medium-high speed until combined but not creamed. The sugar should look moist, crumbly, and purple.

Add the eggs and ube paste and beat on medium speed until combined, about 30 seconds. Add the buttermilk and oil and beat until combined, about 30 seconds.

Sift in half of the flour mixture and whisk by hand until just combined. Repeat with the remaining flour mixture and whisk until just combined.

Divide the batter evenly between the prepared cake pans (about 35 oz./ 990 g each). Bake until a toothpick inserted into the center of the cakes comes out clean, 35 to 40 minutes.

Transfer the pans to a wire rack and let cool for 10 minutes. Run a small offset spatula around the perimeter to loosen the edges. Invert the cakes onto the wire rack. Remove the parchment and invert again onto wire racks so they sit right side up. Let cool completely.

For the coconut frosting: To the bowl of a stand mixer fitted with the paddle, add the sour cream, sugar, and salt. Beat on low speed until combined. Add a third of the coconut and beat on low speed until combined. Repeat two more times.

To assemble: Place one cake layer (top side up) on a cake plate. Top with 2 cups (450 g) of frosting and spread evenly. Top with the second cake layer (bottom side up).

Cover the top evenly with 2½ (560 g) cups of frosting. Use the remaining frosting for the sides. Wrap the cake all over with plastic wrap so it touches the frosting directly and protects the cake from air. Refrigerate overnight. As it sits, both the cake layers and coconut shreds will soak up excess moisture from the frosting.

Let the cake sit out at room temperature for 1 hour to take the chill off before serving. Due to the nature of the frosting, it's best to use a serrated knife to "saw" through the cake into slices. ●

MAKES ONE 9-INCH (23 CM) TWO-LAYER CAKE

Ube Cake

3 cups (375 g) all-purpose flour

1 tablespoon baking powder

1½ teaspoons kosher salt

¾ teaspoon baking soda

¾ cup (186 g) ube halaya, at room temperature

2¼ cups (450 g) granulated sugar

6 large eggs, at room temperature

1 tablespoon ube paste

1½ cups (360 g) buttermilk

1½ cups (315 g) neutral oil

Coconut Frosting

Two 16 oz. (454 g) containers sour cream

4 cups (800 g) granulated sugar

¼ teaspoon kosher salt

14 cups (700 g) unsweetened shredded coconut

I make this for my birthday every year

Cherry Almond Puto Cake

Of all the kakanin (Filipino rice cakes), puto—a fluffy steamed mini muffin—is the least sweet. Its neutral flavor makes it endlessly adaptable as a snack, a side, or a dessert. Puto is traditionally made with rice flour. However, the likes of boxed Bisquick and all-purpose flour have swiftly become popular alternatives, prized for producing a softer and more tender texture. Although cheese and salted eggs are classic embellishments, food coloring is most nostalgic for me since it's how my mom has always made puto special. Growing up, we'd pinch beads of pigment into the mixture, forging different shades from primary colors. After they steamed, my sister and I would arrange the cakes into an edible pastel paint palette.

My version calls on a blend of cake flour and almond flour for a delicate structure and a light, nutty taste. The batter is gathered into one fluffy round, which is extra bouncy, owing to a billow of meringue. Its clean ivory surface is dimpled with sour cherries and almond flakes, creating a mosaic of crimson, cream, and ochre. This makes a light dessert and a quintessential snack cake because it's not too sweet. In the world of Asian desserts, there's no better compliment.

Grease a 9-inch (23 cm) springform pan with cooking spray and line the bottom with parchment paper. Place the prepared pan on a large piece of foil and wrap up the sides tightly (this will catch any unexpected leaking).

Strain the cherries through a fine-mesh sieve, pressing firmly with a rubber spatula to extract as much liquid as possible. This should break up the cherries pretty nicely (if it doesn't, coarsely chop them). Pat with a paper towel several times to eliminate excess moisture (you really want to do a good job of this).

Add water to a 12-inch (30 cm) steamer pot. Cover with a lid (no need for the perforated tier just yet) and bring to a boil over high heat. Reduce to a simmer over low heat. Once it's simmering, stack the perforated tier on top and cover with the lid. Let this hang out while you make the batter.

In a large bowl, whisk together the cake flour, almond flour, ¼ cup (50 g) of the sugar, the baking powder, and salt. Whisk in the milk and almond extract.

To the bowl of a stand mixer fitted with the whisk, add the egg whites and cream of tartar. Beat on medium speed until foamy, about 1 minute. Increase the speed to medium-high and slowly add the remaining ¼ cup (50 g) of sugar (it takes about 30 seconds to add all the sugar). Continue beating until medium-stiff peaks form (peaks should stand up but have a slight curl at the tip), 1 to 3 minutes.

Fold the meringue into the flour mixture in three additions.

Scrape the batter into the prepared pan. Scatter evenly with the cherries and almonds.

(Recipe continued on following page).

MAKES ONE 9-INCH (23 CM) CAKE

⅓ cup (61 g) pitted sour cherries in syrup (see Note)

1½ cups (165 g) cake flour

⅓ cup (26 g) almond flour

½ cup (100 g) granulated sugar, divided

2 teaspoons baking powder

½ teaspoon kosher salt

⅔ cup plus 3 tablespoons (205 g) whole milk

2 teaspoons almond extract

4 large egg whites, at room temperature

¼ teaspoon cream of tartar

1 tablespoon (9 g) sliced almonds

Special Equipment

12-inch (30 cm) steamer (see Note)

Notes: I recommend sour cherries that come in a jar, rather than those that come in a can.

Both metal and bamboo steamers work fine here. When using metal, I wrap the lid in a tea towel to prevent condensation from dripping off the lid into the steamer tray.

(Cherry Almond Puto Cake continued from previous page).

Place the pan in the steamer basket. Cover with the lid and steam until set and a toothpick inserted in the center of the cake comes out clean, 55 to 60 minutes. (If you see a few stray crumbs, that's okay. But there shouldn't be any sign of raw batter).

Transfer the pan to a wire rack (use tongs or a hand towel; it's hot). Let cool for 20 minutes.

Run a small offset spatula around the perimeter to loosen the edges. Unlatch and remove the springform ring. Slide the cake off the springform base. If the parchment is still attached to the bottom, hold the cake in place and pull away the parchment.

Transfer the cake to a cutting board and slice into small diamond portions. Serve slightly warm or at room temperature. ●

Yakult Leches Cake

This riff on Latin tres leches is a passionate ode to my childhood obsession with Yakult, the Japanese probiotic drink that has stolen hearts across the Asian diaspora. Each toy-size vial is sealed with shiny red foil, which I think is just as satisfying to remove as peeling the plastic off fresh electronics. It's part of the Yakult experience. The drink is added to the batter, straight up. But for the soaking liquid, it's simmered into a lightly thickened glaze before joining its canned companions and flooding the warm pillowy cake. Every possible square inch of this dessert is infused with Yakult's bright lactic flavor. And, well, it's just fantastic.

MAKES ONE 9 × 13-INCH (23 × 33 CM) CAKE

Yakult Leches Soak

Four 2.7 fl. oz. (80 ml) bottles Yakult

4 teaspoons cornstarch

One 12 fl. oz. (354 ml) can evaporated milk

½ cup (160 g) sweetened condensed milk

¼ cup (60 g) heavy cream

Cake

1½ cups (187 g) all-purpose flour

1 tablespoon baking powder

½ teaspoon kosher salt

One 2.7 fl. oz. (80 ml) bottle Yakult

3 tablespoons (45 g) heavy cream

3 large eggs, at room temperature

¾ cup (150 g) granulated sugar

Grated zest of 1 lemon

Topping

1½ cups (360 g) heavy cream, cold

2 tablespoons (25 g) granulated sugar

Grated lemon zest, for garnish

For the yakult leches soak: In a small saucepan, whisk together the Yakult and cornstarch. Bring to a boil over high heat. Reduce to a steady simmer and cook until slightly thickened and pourable, 5 to 6 minutes. Transfer to a 4-cup (1 L) liquid measuring cup. You should have about 1 cup (240 g).

Whisk in the evaporated milk, sweetened condensed milk, and heavy cream. Set aside.

For the cake: Preheat the oven to 350°F (180°C). Grease a 9 × 13-inch (23 × 33 cm) cake pan with cooking spray.

In a medium bowl, whisk together the flour, baking powder, and salt.

In a small liquid measuring cup, whisk together the Yakult and heavy cream.

To the bowl of a stand mixer fitted with the whisk, add the eggs and sugar and beat on medium-high speed until thick, pale, and ribbony, 5 to 7 minutes. Beat in the lemon zest.

With the mixer on the lowest speed, gradually add half the flour mixture and mix until just combined. Add half the Yakult mixture and mix until just combined. Repeat.

Scrape the batter into the prepared pan. Bake until a toothpick inserted into the center of the cake comes out clean, about 20 minutes.

Transfer the pan to a wire rack. Immediately poke the cake all over with a long wooden skewer. Give the Yakult leches soak a quick whisk, then pour it evenly over the cake. Let the cake cool to room temperature. Cover with plastic wrap and refrigerate for at least 6 hours, but overnight is best.

For the topping: In the bowl of a stand mixer fitted with the whisk, beat the heavy cream on medium speed until loose peaks form, 1 to 2 minutes. Add the sugar and continue to beat until fluffy and medium-firm peaks form, 1 to 2 minutes. Don't overbeat or it will appear grainy.

Spread the whipped cream over the cake and garnish with lemon zest. ●

Cherry Blossom Inipit

Inipit translates to "pressed" and is essentially the dessert version of a savory tea sandwich made with panels of fluffy chiffon cake. Yema, a sweetened condensed milk custard, is the classic filling. But you can use anything, really. Fruit jam, chocolate-hazelnut spread, peanut butter, ube halaya, or a personal favorite, cherry blossom. Sakura, or cherry blossom, season was my favorite time of year when I lived in Japan as a child. Life became a fairyland full of pink petals, but only for a moment. It was there that I tasted cherry blossom for the first time. Here, its sweet floral flavor is whipped into velvety cream cheese and spread thickly between plush layers of golden chiffon. The neat slices are tidy enough to eat by hand without making a mess. And they're delicate and lovely, just like the fragile blossoms they come from.

For the cake: Preheat the oven to 350°F (180°C). Grease a 9-inch (23 cm) square cake pan with cooking spray and line the bottom with parchment paper.

In a large bowl, whisk together the egg yolks, ¼ cup (50 g) of sugar, the water, oil, and salt. Sift in the flour and baking powder and whisk until just combined.

To the bowl of a stand mixer fitted with the whisk, add the egg whites and cream of tartar. Beat on medium speed until foamy, about 1 minute. Increase the speed to medium-high and slowly add the remaining ½ cup (100 g) of the sugar (it takes about 1 minute to add all the sugar). Continue beating until stiff peaks form (peaks should stand straight up and not curl at the tip), 3 to 5 minutes.

Fold the meringue into yolk mixture in three additions.

Scrape the batter into the prepared baking pan. Bake until the top is lightly golden and a toothpick inserted into the center of the cake comes out clean, 20 to 25 minutes.

Transfer the pan to a wire rack and let cool for 1 minute. Invert the cake onto the wire rack, remove the parchment, and let cool completely.

Transfer the cake to a cutting board. Using a serrated knife, cut the cake into four squares. Slice the thinnest bit off the top layer of each square (we want to get rid of that sticky golden top "crust" and expose the beautiful blemish-free sponge underneath).

Slice each square horizontally into 2 layers (like you're making two pieces of sandwich bread). Set the tops to the side. Arrange the 4 bottom slices on the cutting board (the side that had contact with the baking pan should be facing up). Set aside while you make the filling.

For the filling: In a large bowl, using a hand mixer, beat the cream cheese and salt until smooth. Add the powdered sugar, jam, and sakura powder. Beat until smooth. Transfer the filling to a large pastry bag.

To assemble: Pipe the filling evenly over the 4 bottom slices (I like to pipe a square border all the way around and then pipe another square inside that one, repeating until it's evenly covered). Spread and smooth with a small offset spatula. Top with the 4 top slices of cake and press gently to create a sandwich.

Using a serrated knife, slice each sandwich into 4 finger sandwiches (wipe the blade with a paper towel between each cut to create clean lines). ●

MAKES 16 SANDWICH CAKES

Cake

4 large eggs, separated, at room temperature

¾ cup (150 g) granulated sugar, divided

⅓ cup (80 g) water

¼ cup (52 g) neutral oil

½ teaspoon kosher salt

1 cup (110 g) cake flour

1½ teaspoons baking powder

¼ teaspoon cream of tartar

Filling

8 oz. (226 g) cream cheese, at room temperature

¼ teaspoon kosher salt

¼ cup (25 g) powdered sugar

¼ cup (80 g) sakura jam (see Note)

4 teaspoons (10 g) sakura powder (see Note)

Note: You can purchase sakura jam and powder (a dehydrated form of sakura) online.

Lemongrass Coconut Rose Cake

This is one of those cakes I make often. It's dressy enough for any dinner party, yet casual enough to be that weekend cake that lives on the counter and gradually disappears throughout the day—another chunk missing each time you yourself go back for one more sliver. It's lush with creamy coconut, bright with fresh lemongrass, and faintly floral with a whisper of rose. And it's just really, really good.

The ingredients work intimately together. One stalk of lemongrass steeps in the coconut milk that washes every thing in a tropical flavor. Another stalk is grated and rubbed into the sugar by hand, infusing every grain with its brilliant citrusy tone. It's simultaneously simple and complex. But the texture deserves just as much praise. It's fluffy, downy, and unbelievably moist.

For the cake: Slice one stalk of lemongrass into small rounds and add to a small saucepan along with the coconut milk and water. Bring to a boil over high heat. Reduce to a very gentle simmer and cook, letting the flavors infuse, for 5 minutes. Turn off the heat, cover with a lid, and let steep for 10 minutes.

Strain the mixture through a fine-mesh sieve into a liquid measuring cup. You should have 1 cup (240 g). If you have more, return the liquid to the saucepan and continue to gently simmer uncovered until you have the correct amount. If you have less, add a bit of water. Transfer 4 teaspoons (20 g) to a medium bowl (this is for the glaze). Let cool to room temperature, about 30 minutes.

Meanwhile, preheat the oven to 350°F (180°C). Grease a 9-inch (23 cm) round cake pan with cooking spray and line the bottom with parchment paper.

In a medium bowl, whisk together the flour, baking powder, and salt.

To the bowl of a stand mixer, add the sugar and grate the remaining stalk of lemongrass over top (I generally give up on the last few inches). Rub together with your fingers until moist and fragrant. Lock the bowl into the stand mixer and attach the paddle. Add the butter and beat on medium-high speed until fluffy, about 3 minutes.

Beat in the eggs one at a time. Beat in the rose water. With the mixer on the lowest speed, gradually add half of the flour mixture and mix until just combined. Add half of the infused coconut milk and mix until just combined. Repeat.

Scrape the batter into the prepared pan. Bake until golden brown around the perimeter and a toothpick inserted into the center of the cake comes out clean, 30 to 35 minutes.

Transfer the pan to a wire rack and let cool for 15 minutes. Run a small offset spatula around the perimeter to loosen the edges. Invert the cake onto the wire rack. Remove the parchment. Invert again onto another wire rack so it sits right side up. Let cool completely before transferring to a cake plate.

For the glaze: In the medium bowl with the 4 teaspoons of infused coconut milk, whisk in the powdered sugar, water, and rose water. The glaze should drip off the whisk thick and slow.

Pour the glaze onto the cake, right in the center. Spread evenly but not quite to the edge. Let gravity pull a few thin lazy drips over the sides. Sprinkle with the toasted coconut and rose petals.

You can eat this right away while the glaze is glossy and moist or after it sets (which will happen over the next couple of hours). ●

MAKES ONE 9-INCH (23 CM) CAKE

Cake

2 stalks lemongrass, trimmed and first one or two woody layers removed (about 50 g), divided

1 cup (240 g) canned unsweetened coconut milk

¼ cup (60 g) water

1¾ cups (219 g) all-purpose flour

1½ teaspoons baking powder

½ teaspoon kosher salt

1 cup (200 g) granulated sugar

1 stick (113 g) unsalted butter, at room temperature

3 large eggs, at room temperature

½ teaspoon rose water

Glaze and Garnish

1 cup (100 g) powdered sugar

½ teaspoon water

¼ teaspoon rose water

Unsweetened shredded coconut, toasted, for garnish

Dried culinary rose petals, for garnish

Pineapple Guava Mamon Cupcakes

My first New York apartment was on 69th Street on the Upper West Side. If you headed east, you'd hit Central Park. But if you walked in the opposite direction, you could step right inside the doors of Magnolia Bakery, parked on the corner of Columbus. I must have gone there every night during my first two weeks. I'd wait in line (there's always a line), eyes fixed on the glass cabinet trimmed with tiny cakes, all frosted with Magnolia's famous signature swirl.

Filipino bakeries across the globe sell mamon, small rounds of chiffon often served plain and buttered, or in colorful flavors like pandan, ube, and mocha. They're as cute as a cupcake, hence my appendage of frosting. These plush and airy cakes are flavored with sweet golden pineapple and fruity pink guava. You can frost these cupcakes any way you like, with a piping tip or a carefree swish-and-swipe. But I prefer to frost mine Magnolia-style, with a captivating clear curl carved into the center.

For the cupcakes: Preheat the oven to 350°F (180°C). Line 18 cups of two 12-cup muffin tins with cupcake liners.

In a large bowl, whisk together the egg yolks, ¼ cup (50 g) of the sugar, the pineapple juice, oil, and salt. Sift in the flour and baking powder and whisk until just combined.

To the bowl of a stand mixer fitted with the whisk, add the egg whites and cream of tartar and beat on medium speed until foamy, about 1 minute. Increase the speed to medium-high and slowly add the remaining ½ cup (100 g) of the sugar (it takes about 1 minute to add all the sugar). Continue beating until stiff peaks form (peaks should stand straight up and not curl at the tip), 3 to 5 minutes.

Fold the meringue into the pineapple mixture in three additions.

Divide the batter evenly among the cupcake liners (I like using an ice cream scoop for this), about 4 heaping tablespoons each.

Bake until golden and a toothpick inserted into the center of the cupcakes comes out clean, about 10 minutes.

Transfer the pans to a wire rack and let cool for 1 minute. Transfer the cupcakes to the wire rack and let cool completely.

For the frosting: In a small saucepan, add the guava paste and guava concentrate and cook over medium-low heat, first breaking up the paste with a whisk and then whisking constantly until combined and the mixture resembles a thick puree, about 5 minutes. (A few bubbles are okay, but this shouldn't simmer).

Transfer to a liquid measuring cup. You should have about ½ cup (138 g). Let cool to room temperature, stirring occasionally. Do not refrigerate or it will become too thick.

(Recipe continued on the following page).

MAKES 18 CUPCAKES

Cupcakes

4 large eggs, separated, at room temperature

¾ cup (150 g) granulated sugar, divided

⅓ cup (80 g) pineapple juice

¼ cup (52 g) neutral oil

½ teaspoon kosher salt

1 cup (110 g) cake flour

1½ teaspoons baking powder

¼ teaspoon cream of tartar

Frosting and Garnish

4 oz. (113 g) guava paste, cubed

⅓ cup (80 g) guava concentrate (such as Dafruta)

½ cup (120 g) heavy cream, cold

8 oz. (226 g) mascarpone

2 tablespoons (12 g) powdered sugar

Pinch of kosher salt

Coarsely crushed freeze-dried pineapple, for garnish

(Pineapple Guava Mamon Cupcakes continued from previous page).

In a large bowl, using a hand mixer, beat the heavy cream on medium-high speed until stiff peaks form, about 3 minutes. Transfer to a small bowl and set aside.

In the same large bowl (no need to clean), beat the mascarpone, powdered sugar, and salt on medium speed until just combined. Do not overmix. Add the cooled guava mixture and beat on low speed until mostly combined but not quite. Finishing mixing with a rubber spatula. Fold in the whipped cream in two additions.

To assemble: Scoop 2 tablespoons of the frosting onto each of the cooled cupcakes. Spread with a small offset spatula, forming a circular swirl like you're carving out a small crater in the center. Garnish with the crushed freeze-dried pineapple. ●

Brown Sugar, Orange & Cardamom Cassava Cake

This isn't your typical cake. Instead of flour, it's made with grated cassava (aka yuca), a starchy root vegetable. The cake is squishy and chewy, but not quite as gummy as a glutinous rice cake. The surface, covered with a layer of custard, is mottled with dark charred spots from several minutes under the broiler. Altogether it's creamy and comforting.

My family always made it with one can each of coconut, condensed, and evaporated milk. But my version calls for just two cans of coconut milk—one for the cake and the other for the custard topping. It's lighter but just as satisfyingly lush. Orange juice and zest bring a burst of brightness. Cardamom adds a layer of warmth. And the brown sugar coats it all in a toasty sweetness. If you feel passionate about grating fresh yuca root by hand, just be sure to wring out the excess moisture. But I usually (read: always) buy it frozen and grated.

Preheat the oven to 350°F (180°C). Grease a 9-inch (23 cm) square cake pan with cooking spray and line with parchment paper so there is overhang on two sides.

In a large bowl, whisk together one can of the coconut milk, the whole eggs, 1 cup (200 g) of the brown sugar, the orange zest, orange juice, cardamom, vanilla, and salt. Whisk in the cassava.

Scrape the batter into the prepared pan. Bake until the top is no longer glossy, the edges are golden, and a toothpick inserted into the center of the cake comes out mostly clean with a few sticky crumbs, about 1 hour. Remove the cake from the oven (but leave the oven on).

In a medium bowl, whisk together the remaining can of coconut milk, remaining ¼ cup (50 g) of brown sugar, the egg yolks, and cornstarch.

Pour over the warm cake. Return to the oven and continue to bake until the custard has thickened but still jiggles, about 20 minutes.

Turn on the broiler (select high if it's an option and leave the cake on the center rack). Broil until deeply golden in spots, about 5 minutes (this will depend on the strength of your broiler). Move the pan around as needed to toast evenly. Keep in mind the custard will still be jiggly but will set as it cools.

Transfer the pan to a wire rack and let cool completely before covering with foil. Refrigerate until chilled, at least 6 hours, but overnight is best.

Run a small offset spatula around the perimeter to loosen the edges. Using the parchment overhang as handles, lift the cake onto a cutting board. Slice into portions (I usually cut 16 portions). Serve chilled, at room temperature, or slightly heated. ●

MAKES ONE 9-INCH (23 CM) SQUARE CAKE

Two 13.5 fl. oz. (400 ml) cans unsweetened coconut milk, divided

2 large eggs

1¼ cups (250 g) light brown sugar, divided

Grated zest of 1 orange

4 teaspoons (35 g) fresh orange juice

½ teaspoon ground cardamom

½ teaspoon vanilla bean paste or extract

¼ teaspoon kosher salt

One 16 oz. (450 g) package frozen grated cassava (yuca), thawed

2 large egg yolks

4 teaspoons cornstarch

Buttermilk Berry Bibingka

I made a lot of boxed cakes when I was a kid. There was something about walking down the baking aisle surrounded by printed pictures of perfectly frosted, thick layer cakes that always inspired me to go home and make a mess in my family's kitchen. And although my creations never turned out like the photos, I was still very particular when it came to my prepackaged blends. Always Duncan Hines for fudgy brownies and always Betty Crocker for vanilla cake. But there was another brand found only at our local Asian market—White King, which promised the tastiest bibingka.

Bibingka is a Filipino rice cake, baked in fragrant banana leaves, and garnished with anything from melty cheese, to salted eggs, to macapuno (jarred coconut strings), or coconut flakes. It's a classic holiday treat, very popular during the Christmas season. The versatility of bibingka isn't limited to the toppings. Some use coconut milk in the batter. Others, whole milk. And there are those who like to include condensed milk for an extra layer of sweetness. Bibingka is always made with rice flour—either regular, glutinous, or a combination of the two. Regular rice flour creates a delicate texture, while glutinous rice flour (also called sweet rice flour) creates a mochi-level chew with a tight and stretchy crumb. I like to cut regular rice flour with a bit of all-purpose flour (which really fluffs up the texture).

What truly sets my version apart from the rest is buttermilk, which adds extra moisture and a cool tang. Before the cake is finished baking, whole berries are scattered over the top and nestle into the surface creating a patchwork of scarlet and sapphire. It's fresh and fruity, lightly sweetened, and balanced with the comforting taste of rice. Like some of my childhood masterpieces, this bibingka doesn't look anything like the one on the box. But I can promise you that it is delicious.

MAKES ONE 9-INCH (23 CM) CAKE

Thawed frozen banana leaf, cut into a 13-inch (33 cm) round (optional)

1½ cups (360 g) buttermilk, at room temperature

1½ cups (300 g) granulated sugar

6 tablespoons (84 g) unsalted butter, melted

1 large egg, at room temperature

1 teaspoon vanilla bean paste or extract

1¼ cups (137 g) rice flour

½ cup (62 g) all-purpose flour

2 teaspoons baking powder

½ teaspoon kosher salt

¼ teaspoon baking soda

8 oz (225 g) mixed fresh berries (about 1½ cups)

Preheat the oven to 375°F (190°C).

Press the banana leaf into a 9-inch (23 cm) round cake pan. (Alternatively, grease the pan with cooking spray and line the bottom with parchment paper).

In a large bowl, whisk together the buttermilk, sugar, melted butter, egg, and vanilla. Whisk in the rice flour, all-purpose flour, baking powder, salt, and baking soda. The batter will be fairly loose.

Pour the batter into the prepared pan. Bake until the surface is just beginning to form a skin in places, 15 to 20 minutes. Remove the cake from the oven (but leave the oven on).

Add a berry to the center. If it doesn't immediately sink to the bottom, go ahead and scatter all the berries over top. If the test berry sinks, return to the oven and bake for another 5 minutes before testing again. (Ultimately, some of the berries will sink to the bottom. But they shouldn't all disappear).

Continue to bake until a toothpick inserted into the center of the cake comes out mostly clean with a few sticky crumbs, 35 to 40 minutes.

Transfer the pan to a wire rack and let cool for 15 minutes. Run a small offset spatula around the perimeter to loosen the edges. Invert the cake onto the wire rack. Remove the banana leaf or parchment. Invert again onto another wire rack so it sits right side up. Serve warm or at room temperature. ●

Vanilla of the East

The islands that make up the Philippines—with their crystal water beaches, glorious golden sun, and green jungles—are a treasure trove of some of the world's most magnificent ingredients. A tropical paradise of flavor. Brilliant fruits, flowers, and nuts hang in the air, filling the atmosphere with sweet perfume, and illuminating the land with more colors than an artist's palette. Many of these treasures have made their way into mainstream Western cooking, prompting food trends and media write-ups, and appearing in bakeries and food publications. Coconut, rice, lemongrass, even ube, the purple yam, fall somewhere on the spectrum of ordinary to novelty. But (at least for now) there's one ingredient I find underrated on this side of the globe: pandan—an emerald-green shrub with long blade-shaped leaves. Otherwise known as "vanilla of the East."

Vanilla can work quietly in the background. But pandan doesn't whisper the same way.

While pandan might be as common in Southeast Asia as vanilla is everywhere else, I don't treat them with the same regard. The creamy, sweet, and musky essence of vanilla fits reasonably into to almost every dessert. Even when it's not the leading flavor, vanilla can work quietly in the background. But pandan doesn't whisper the same way. It's detectable, even in the faintest amounts, and wields an elusive flavor and fragrance that's altogether grassy (but not bitter), nutty (think almond and coconut), and sweet (resembling vanilla and rose). Pandan is richly pigmented and, when in a liquid state, stains everything it touches with mystical green hues. I may very well toss vanilla around with reckless abandon. But when it comes to pandan, I'm intentional.

This tropical plant, used in both sweet and savory dishes, is often found in the freezer section of Asian supermarkets. Fresh leaves can be stirred into puddings, creams, and curries. Or treated as a wrapper for meats and rice. But perhaps my favorite way to use pandan is to blitz the leaves with water and strain it, forging a gem-colored elixir ready to infuse anything from cake batters to pastry fillings. There really isn't anything like it (which is why I don't recommend substitutes other than commercial pastes and extracts). For such distinct and unique qualities, pandan is incredibly versatile and pairs beautifully with a wide range of flavors.

In this book, you'll find pandan baked into the layers of my **Raspberry Buko Pandan Cake** (page 24) where it's lifted by bright pops of fruity tartness. It joins the deep notes of dark chocolate and coffee in my **Southeast Tiramisu** (page 142). And it adds sweet and earthy tropical notes to my creamy **Pandan Coconut Cream Pie** (page 102). If you've tasted pandan, then you already know the extent of its magnificence. If you haven't, then you're genuinely in for a revelation. ●

02

Cookies
& Bars

Hibiscus Jackfruit Uraro Cookies

Uraro cookies are sold in bakeries across the Philippine islands but hail from southern Luzon. They're made with arrowroot starch, which gives them a fine, delicate, melt-in-your-mouth texture. Like butter spritz cookies, the dough is soft and creamy, and often baked into patterned rounds, flowers, or stars. I use a cookie press with a flower disc. But a large piping bag with a large star tip works well here, too.

My version looks and tastes like the vibrant petals of my favorite tropical flower—hibiscus, which blossom in multicolor tones across my family's compound in the Philippines. Here, sweet and musky jackfruit counters the puckery tartness of hibiscus, while the gentle taste of butter lingers in the background. I favor using arrowroot starch and all-purpose flour in equal parts. This strengthens the cookie's fragile structure, while still maintaining the powdery texture uraro is known for.

Preheat the oven to 350°F (180°C).

In a large bowl, using a hand mixer, beat together the butter, powdered sugar, and salt on low speed until creamy and combined, 1 to 2 minutes. Beat in the egg yolk.

Sift in the arrowroot flour, all-purpose flour, and baking powder. Beat on low speed until it forms a soft dough.

Transfer one-third of the dough (about ⅓ cup or 110 g) to a small bowl.

To the larger portion of dough, add the jackfruit paste and beat on low speed until combined.

In a pinch bowl, whisk together the hibiscus powder and boiling water. Add to the smaller portion of dough, along with the food coloring (if using), and beat on low speed until combined.

Fasten a flower disc onto a cookie press. Fill with 2 tablespoons of jackfruit dough, then 1 tablespoon of hibiscus dough. Repeat this scooping sequence two more times.

Press the dough into cookies onto an ungreased sheet pan, spacing them 1 inch (2.5 cm) apart (these won't spread much).

Bake until dry and set (don't let them get brown), about 15 minutes.

Transfer the pan to a wire rack and let cool for 5 minutes. Transfer the cookies to the wire rack and let cool completely.

Repeat with the remaining dough, refilling the cookie press with the same scooping sequence and using a fresh ungreased sheet pan. ●

MAKES ABOUT 40 COOKIES

1 stick (113 g) unsalted butter, at room temperature

½ cup (50 g) powdered sugar

¼ teaspoon kosher salt

1 large egg yolk, at room temperature

½ cup plus 2 tablespoons (82 g) arrowroot flour

½ cup plus 2 tablespoons (78 g) all-purpose flour

½ teaspoon baking powder

½ teaspoon jackfruit paste

1 teaspoon hibiscus powder

1 teaspoon (5 g) boiling water

3 drops purple gel food coloring (optional; see Note)

Special Equipment

Cookie press with flower disc

Note: I use the color Fuchsia by Chefmaster.

Coconut Almond Raspberry Polvoron

We always had polvoron in our snack cupboard when I was a kid, right next to the Oreos, the Goldfish, and Lay's. I'd reach my hand into the glass jar my mom kept them in, listening for the sound, rather than the feel, to let me know I had one in my grip. Wrapped individually in glossy neon cellophane, twisted tightly at opposite ends like bubble gum candy, they'd let out a loud articulate crinkle with even the slightest touch.

This shortbread cookie is one of many Filipino dishes with Spanish roots. Polvo translates to "powder" in Spanish, alluding to its texture, which is very crumbly. Each bite leaves behind a pile of soft sugary dust on your tongue.

My recipe uses a blend of almond and coconut flour (instead of all-purpose) for a nutty tropical flavor I like even better than the original. The freeze-dried raspberries add a pop of fruitiness that cuts through the buttery richness. If giving as pasalubong (gifts), you can package these in colorful tissue paper or simply nest them inside ribbed cupcake liners. But for top-tier ASMR quality, cello wrap is the way to go.

MAKES 24 SMALL COOKIES

½ cup (55 g) coconut flour

1 cup (80 g) milk powder

½ cup (40 g) almond flour

⅓ cup (66 g) granulated sugar

1 oz. (28 g) package freeze-dried raspberries, ground into a powder

⅛ teaspoon kosher salt

1 stick (113 g) unsalted butter

Special Equipment

24-cavity bite-size brownie silicone mold (see Note)

Note: You can purchase bite-size brownie molds online or in craft stores. Alternatively, use a mini cupcake tin lined with paper liners.

In a medium nonstick skillet, toast the coconut flour over medium heat, stirring regularly, until fragrant and golden, about 3 minutes.

Transfer the toasted coconut flour to a large bowl and whisk in the milk powder, almond flour, sugar, raspberry powder, and salt.

In the same skillet, melt the butter over medium-low heat. Pour over the flour mixture. Stir with a fork, mashing the butter into the mixture, until well combined.

Divide the mixture among the 24 cavities of a bite-size brownie silicone mold and press firmly with a spoon or small wooden dowel, compacting the mixture. You'll need to do this in batches. Start with 3 heaping teaspoons per cavity, pack down, and go from there.

Freeze until firm, about 30 minutes. Remove from the molds.

To give as pasalubong (gifts), wrap in colorful cellophane paper or set inside cupcake molds and enclose in a treat box. Store in the freezer or refrigerator. ●

Silvana Macarons

These macarons are inspired by silvanas, cashew meringue sand-wich cookies filled and slathered with French buttercream and coated in graham cracker crumbs. Here, a heap of graham cracker dust is folded right into the frosting—rich and unctuous due to all the egg yolks—where it softens and fades into the silky spread, imparting its signature flavor. A hearty dollop is pressed between two nutty cashew meringue wafers. It's crisp and chewy and creamy. You can eat these chilled, but I like them straight from the freezer, just like silvanas.

For the meringue wafers: Line two sheet pans with a silicone macaron mat (I like the kind where each round has 3 concentric circles and a single dot in the center).

In a large bowl, whisk together the powdered sugar and cashew flour.

In the bowl of a stand mixer fitted with the whisk, beat the egg whites and salt on medium speed until foamy, about 1 minute. Increase the speed to medium-high and slowly add the sugar (it takes about 90 seconds to add all the sugar). Continue beating until stiff peaks form (peaks should stand straight up and not curl at the tip), about 2 minutes.

Sift the cashew mixture over the meringue. Combine, folding gently with a spatula, until the mixture falls off the spatula in a slow, thick ribbon (this takes about 30 strokes). Transfer the mixture to a large piping bag fitted with a ½-inch (1.25 cm) round tip (Wilton #1A).

Using the smallest circle on the macaron mats as a guide (which has a 1 ¼-inch [3.25 cm] diameter), pipe 30 rounds of the batter until it fills the circle. Be steady and confident about it, pulling the piping bag straight up as you finish filling each circle. The tip will flop over like a tail, but the batter will spread evenly to fill the largest circle on the macaron mats (which has a 1 ¾-inch [4.5 cm] diameter).

Gently tap the sheet pan against the counter to eliminate air bubbles. Use a toothpick to work out any remaining air bubbles. Sprinkle with the graham cracker crumbs. Let rest for 1 hour to allow the batter to form a skin and turn from shiny to matte.

Meanwhile, preheat the oven to 300°F (150°C).

Bake one pan at a time until the tops are dry and the wafers have risen and formed a bubbly, ruffled base (this is called a "foot"), 12 to 15 minutes. Transfer the pan to a wire rack. Let cool completely before carefully peeling the wafers away from the silicone mat.

For the French graham buttercream: In the bowl of a stand mixer fitted with the whisk, whisk the egg yolks on medium-high speed until thick and pale, about 4 minutes.

In a small saucepan, add the sugar and water. Cook over low heat, whisking until the sugar is dissolved, 2 to 3 minutes.

Increase the heat to medium-high and bring to a boil. Cook, without stir-ring, until an instant-read thermometer registers 240°F (115°C), about 30 seconds (this can happen extremely fast, so check the temperature as soon as it boils).

MAKES 15 MACARONS

Meringue Wafers

2 cups (200 g) powdered sugar

1 cup plus 1 tablespoon (110 g) finely ground cashew flour (see Note)

3 large egg whites, at room temperature

Pinch of fine sea salt

¼ cup (50 g) granulated sugar

2 tablespoons (12 g) finely ground graham cracker crumbs

French Graham Buttercream

5 large egg yolks, at room temperature

⅓ cup plus 2 tablespoons (90 g) granulated sugar

2 tablespoons (30 g) water

2 sticks (226 g) unsalted butter, at room temperature

½ cup (50 g) finely ground graham cracker crumbs

1 teaspoon vanilla extract

Pinch of fine sea salt

Special Equipment

Silicone macaron mat (see Note)

Notes: You can purchase cashew flour online or at natural foods stores. But you can also make your own by pulsing whole cashews (don't overdo it or you'll make cashew butter) and sifting it through a fine-mesh sieve.

If you don't have a macaron mat, line two sheet pans with parchment paper. If you really want to be meticulous, you can use a 1 ¼-inch (3.25 cm) round cutter to trace circles onto the parchment. Flip the parchment upside down so you don't transfer any pencil graphite to the batter.

Turn the stand mixer back on to medium-high speed and very slowly drizzle in the hot sugar syrup (it takes about 1 minute to add all the syrup). Continue beating until the mixture is pale, fluffy, and has cooled to room temperature, about 8 minutes.

With the mixer still running, gradually add the butter, 2 tablespoons at a time, letting it incorporate before adding more (it takes 2 to 3 minutes to add all the butter). The mixture may thin out, look curdled, or both as you add the butter. But don't worry!

Continue beating until the mixture is smooth and creamy and collects on the whisk, 3 to 4 minutes. Don't overwhip or it will split.

Turn off the mixer. Fold in the graham cracker crumbs, vanilla, and salt by hand.

To assemble: Transfer the buttercream to a large piping bag and cut off a large tip. Pipe a dollop of the buttercream onto the bottom of half of the meringue wafers. Gently sandwich together with the rest of the meringue wafers.

If not eating right away, refrigerate in an airtight container for up to 7 days. You can also freeze these for a longer shelf life and eat them straight from the freezer. ●

You can eat these chilled, but I like them straight from the freezer, just like silvanas.

Ube Milk Crinkles

Goldilocks, a beloved Philippine bakery with several Stateside out-posts, refers to ube crinkles as a "classic-in-the-making." It's not a traditional cookie with a long-standing history (neither my mom nor my Lola ate them growing up), but nonetheless, they're here to stay.

These have a crispy crackly exterior and fudgy middles, owing to melted butter and just enough flour to pull the dough together. Instead of powdered sugar, the tops are painted with melted white chocolate, which I know gets a lot of flak for not really being choco-late. In reality, it probably shouldn't even be thought of that way. It's more like milk in a solid form. And it adds a cozy lingering dairy fla-vor to these cookies. Not to mention, it creates a striking two-tone crinkle effect. Combined with the sweet and nutty flavor of ube, these cookies taste like they've been dunked into a glass of milk.

In a medium bowl, whisk together the flour, baking powder, and salt.

In a large bowl, using a hand mixer, beat the cooled melted butter and sugar on medium-high speed until well combined, about 1 minute (remem-ber the butter is melted so this will be looser than creamed softened butter and sugar).

Add the ube halaya and milk powder and beat until well combined, about 30 seconds. Add the egg and ube paste and beat until well combined (it's okay if it looks a little curdled).

Add the flour mixture all at once and beat on low speed until mostly combined but not quite. Finish mixing with a rubber spatula. Cover the bowl with plastic wrap and refrigerate until firm, at least 3 hours and up to overnight.

When you're ready to bake, use a 1½-tablespoon scoop to scoop mounds of the dough onto a parchment-lined sheet pan. Smash and shape each mound into a 2-inch (5 cm) disc. If things get sticky, dust your hands as needed with extra flour (but don't overdo it).

Toss the discs in the extra sugar until coated and transfer to a dinner plate (this will take up less space in the refrigerator). Chill for 15 minutes.

Meanwhile, preheat the oven to 350°F (180°C).

In a small heatproof bowl, add the white chocolate and microwave in 15-second increments, whisking in between, until melted and smooth.

Transfer 8 chilled dough discs to the parchment-lined sheet pan (alternating three rows of 2 with two rows of 1).

Using a small offset spatula, spread a layer of the melted white chocolate on top of the dough discs. Add a few random vertical swipes on the sides.

Bake until the tops are cracked and the edges are firm, 12 to 13 minutes.

Transfer the pan to a wire rack and let cool for 5 minutes. Transfer the cook-ies to the wire rack and let cool completely.

Repeat with the remaining dough, using a fresh parchment-lined sheet pan and microwaving the white chocolate for another 15 seconds or so to thin it out. ●

MAKES ABOUT 20 COOKIES

1¼ cups (156 g) all-purpose flour, plus extra for dusting

1 teaspoon baking powder

¼ teaspoon kosher salt

1 stick (113 g) unsalted butter, melted and cooled completely

⅔ cup (133 g) granulated sugar, plus extra for rolling

½ cup (124 g) ube halaya, at room temperature

1 tablespoon (7 g) malted milk powder

1 large egg, at room tempera-ture

1 teaspoon ube paste

75 g white chocolate, finely chopped (about ⅓ cup)

Kumquat Curd Bars

I eagerly await kumquat season every year. They're brilliantly citrusy, very tart, and sweet, like an ambrosial orange. Kumquats are meant to be eaten whole. Most of the sugar is actually concentrated in the peel, while the tartness lies in its juicy flesh. So, you really need both elements to get the full sweet-and-sour experience. These custardy bars, made with whole kumquats, glow like the orange that paints the morning sky. And they taste like a drink of sunshine, bright and beaming.

For the crust: Preheat the oven to 350°F (180°C). Grease an 8-inch (20 cm) square cake pan with cooking spray and line with parchment paper so there is overhang on two sides.

In a food processor, add the flour, powdered sugar, and salt. Pulse to combine. Add the butter and run the motor until the flour absorbs the butter and the mixture looks crumbly.

Scatter the mixture evenly into the prepared pan and press firmly into the bottom.

Bake until golden brown around the perimeter, about 25 minutes. Transfer the pan to a wire rack.

Reduce the oven temperature to 300°F (150°C).

For the filling: Slice the kumquats in half and remove the seeds. Add to a food processor along with the sugar, butter, and salt. Process until smooth. Add the eggs and cornstarch and pulse until combined. Pour the mixture over the crust.

Return to the oven and bake until the filling is just set and does not jiggle, 25 to 30 minutes. Transfer the pan to a wire rack and let cool completely. Cover with foil and refrigerate until chilled, at least 6 hours, but overnight is best.

Using the parchment overhang as handles, lift the chilled square onto a cutting board. Slice into 9 squares. Then cut each square in half to make 18 long petite bars. ●

MAKES 18 BARS

Crust

1 cup (125 g) all-purpose flour

½ cup (50 g) powdered sugar

¼ teaspoon kosher salt

1 stick (113 g) cold unsalted butter, cubed

Filling

5¼ oz. (150 g) kumquats (about 18), rinsed, dried, and stems removed

¾ cup (150 g) granulated sugar

4 tablespoons (56 g) unsalted butter, at room temperature

⅛ teaspoon kosher salt

3 large eggs, at room temperature

4 teaspoons cornstarch

Chili Crisp Chocolate Chunk Cookies

Fellow members of the chili crisp fan club will revel in these umami-packed cookies where sweet and savory battle deliciously for attention. These are gooey, mottled with melty pools of dark chocolate, and wrinkled with crunchy golden ridges. Brown butter makes them toasty, nutty, and extra chewy. But it's the chili crisp that really gives these cookies that *je ne sais quoi*. Any brand of chili crisp will do, but I prefer the OG Lao Gan Ma for that perfect hit of MSG.

In a small saucepan, heat the butter over medium heat, stirring occasionally, until melted and it turns toasty and brown, about 5 minutes.

Transfer the brown butter to the bowl of a stand mixer and let cool to room temperature, about 45 minutes.

In a medium bowl, whisk together the flour, baking powder, and baking soda.

Lock the bowl into the stand mixer and attach the paddle. Add the brown sugar, granulated sugar, egg, and salt. Beat on medium-high speed until pale, creamy, and the paddle leaves behind ripples in the mixture, about 2 minutes. Beat in the chili crisp and vanilla.

Add the flour mixture all at once and beat on the lowest speed until almost combined but not quite. Add the chocolate and beat until just combined.

Transfer the dough to a medium bowl. Cover with plastic wrap and refrigerate for at least 2 hours and up to overnight.

When you're ready to bake, preheat the oven to 350°F (180°C).

Using a 1½-tablespoon scoop, scoop 9 mounds of dough onto a parchment-lined sheet pan. (Keep the remaining dough in the refrigerator). Sprinkle with red pepper flakes, pressing them on gently to make them stick.

Bake until puffed and light golden around the edges, 10 to 12 minutes. Transfer the pan to a wire rack and let cool for 5 minutes. Transfer the cookies to the wire rack and let cool for at least another 5 minutes. You can enjoy these warm or let them cool completely.

Repeat with the remaining dough, using a fresh parchment-lined sheet pan. ●

MAKES 18 TO 20 COOKIES

1 stick (113 g) unsalted butter

1¼ cups (156 g) all-purpose flour

½ teaspoon baking powder

½ teaspoon baking soda

⅔ cup (133 g) dark brown sugar

¼ cup (50 g) granulated sugar

1 large egg, at room temperature

¾ teaspoon kosher salt

2 teaspoons (10 g) chili crisp (see Note)

1 teaspoon vanilla extract

One 3.5 oz. (100 g) bar dark chocolate (70% cacao), chopped (about ⅔ cup)

Red pepper flakes, for sprinkling

Note: When scooping the chili crisp, try to avoid the oil and get mostly the crisp part.

Red Bean Brownies

I can see how beans in dessert might seem questionable to those who have never tried it. But as millions of people across Asia can attest, it works. In Filipino cuisine, sweetened red beans are a standard ingredient for many desserts, like hopia, buchi, and frozen ice buko. And they're featured prominently in these glossy decadent brownies. To be clear, this is not the type of recipe that attempts to fake you out by covering up beans with copious amounts of sugar and chocolate. The beans are the star, adding an earthy creaminess that makes these brownies fudgy, moist, and irresistible. The batter comes together effortlessly in a food processor and you don't need to worry about overmixing because it's unintentionally gluten-free. This one's a sleeper.

MAKES 16 BROWNIES

One 15 oz. (430 g) can sweetened red bean paste, such as Morinaga

2 large eggs, cold

⅓ cup (66 g) granulated sugar

¼ cup (25 g) unsweetened Dutch process cocoa powder

2 tablespoons (26 g) neutral oil

1 tablespoon vanilla extract

1½ teaspoons malted milk powder

¾ teaspoon kosher salt

Preheat the oven to 350°F (180°C). Grease an 8-inch (20 cm) square cake pan with cooking spray and line with parchment paper so there is overhang on two sides.

In a food processor, add the sweetened red bean paste, eggs, sugar, cocoa powder, oil, vanilla, malted milk powder, and salt. Process until smooth and combined.

Scrape the batter into the prepared pan and spread into an even layer. Bake until the top is dry and an instant-read thermometer inserted into the center of the brownies registers 205°F (96°C), about 30 minutes.

Transfer the pan to a wire rack and let cool for at least 30 minutes. Using the parchment overhang as handles, lift the brownie onto a cutting board. Cut into 16 squares.

Cover with plastic wrap and store in the refrigerator. ●

Island Sunset Sugar Cookies

One of my most vivid memories of visiting the Philippines was watching the sunset night after night. As dusk approached, my cousins and I would run out to the nipa hut (a bamboo shelter on stilts) in the palay (rice field), where we'd climb and play and just be kids. I remember looking straight up at the sky, washed with pink and orange and gold, and thinking if it fell down all around us, that would be okay with me.

These soft, chewy cookies are inspired by those evenings, where the air glowed with ethereal splendor, and everything in the world felt right. The coconut-scented dough is split and flavored with mango, passion fruit, and guava, and then reunited in each round cookie. Don't worry about being too delicate when merging the different doughs together. Aim to swirl and blend the colors more than you would for a Neapolitan design. The cookies will look a little puffed when they come out of the oven, but will settle as they cool, creating squishy middles that taste bright and juicy.

MAKES 20 COOKIES

2½ cups (312 g) all-purpose flour

¾ teaspoon baking soda

½ teaspoon baking powder

½ teaspoon kosher salt

2 sticks (226 g) unsalted butter, at room temperature

1 cup (200 g) granulated sugar

¼ cup (50 g) light brown sugar

1 large egg, at room temperature

1 teaspoon coconut extract

3 tablespoons (15 g) mango powder (from freeze-dried)

5 drops yellow gel food coloring (optional; see Note)

3 tablespoons (18 g) passion fruit powder

5 drops orange gel food coloring (optional; see Note)

2 tablespoons (16 g) guava powder

7 drops pink gel food coloring (optional; see Note)

Note: I use the colors Rose Pink, Sunset Orange, and Golden Yellow by Chefmaster.

Preheat the oven to 350°F (180°C).

In a medium bowl, whisk together the flour, baking soda, baking powder, and salt.

In the bowl of a stand mixer fitted with the paddle, beat the butter, granulated sugar, and brown sugar on medium-high speed until pale and fluffy, 3 to 4 minutes. Beat in the egg and coconut extract until combined, about 30 seconds.

With the mixer on the lowest speed, gradually beat in the flour mixture until just combined. Divide the dough into 4 equal portions (about 205 g each).

Return one portion to the stand mixer bowl. Add the mango powder and yellow food coloring (if using) and mix on low speed until combined. Remove the dough and set aside.

Add another plain portion to the bowl (no need to wipe out). Add the passion fruit powder and orange food coloring (if using) and mix on low speed until combined. Remove the dough and set aside.

Add another plain portion to the bowl (no need to wipe out). Add the guava powder and pink food coloring (if using) and mix on low speed until combined. You should now have three colored doughs and a plain one.

Working with 1 dough at a time, scoop ½-tablespoon (about 10 g) mounds of all 4 doughs onto a parchment-lined sheet pan. Organize the mounds as you scoop, creating 20 piles of dough, each with all four colors. Roll each pile into a single ball, marbling the colors by squishing and manipulating the dough.

Transfer 8 balls to a parchment-lined sheet pan (alternating three rows of 2 with two rows of 1). Bake until puffed and little cracks begin to appear around the edges, 10 to 11 minutes. Do not overbake.

Transfer the pan to a wire rack and let cool for 5 minutes. Transfer the cookies to the wire rack and let cool completely.

Repeat with the remaining dough, using a fresh parchment-lined sheet pan for each batch. ●

Strawberry Rambutan Bars

Rambutan, a fruit cultivated across the tropical countries of Southeast Asia, is in the same family as lychee and longan. And this recipe can, in fact, be made with any of these fruits. Like its cousins, rambutans are fleshy fruits, milky like white opals, enclosed in a firm protective shell. Covered completely in soft spikes, fresh rambutans look like tiny crimson sea urchins. They're delicate and juicy and taste very similar to lychee, though not quite as floral.

Rambutans also carry notes of strawberry. And joining the two amplifies their features while creating layers of flavor and dimension. Once the crust bakes by itself for a bit, it's topped with the filling and the whole thing bakes on a hot sheet pan. This keeps the crust sturdy (and not soggy). The fruit becomes lovely and jammy while the shortbread remains firm and crisp. You can eat these at room temperature or chilled. And I'm honestly not sure which I like better.

For the crust: Preheat the oven to 375°F (190°C). Grease an 8-inch (20 cm) square cake pan with cooking spray and line with parchment paper so there is overhang on two sides.

In a food processor, add the flour, butter, egg yolk, sugar, baking powder, and salt. Pulse a few times, then run the machine until it looks sandy and combined.

Transfer one-third of the mixture (about 1 cup / 140 g) to a small bowl. Squish together with your fingers to create larger dough crumbles. Set aside in the refrigerator.

Scatter the remaining mixture evenly into the prepared pan and press firmly into the bottom.

Bake until golden all over, about 30 minutes. Transfer the pan to a wire rack. Leave the oven on.

Move the oven rack to the lowest position and place a sheet pan on top. Let heat for 15 minutes while the crust cools.

For the strawberry rambutan filling: In a large bowl, stir together the rambutans, strawberries, sugar, cornstarch, lemon zest, lemon juice, and salt. (If you prep this mixture while the crust cools, don't add the sugar until right before you're ready to add the filling to the crust so the fruit doesn't macerate).

To assemble: Spread the strawberry-rambutan mixture over the crust. Sprinkle with the reserved chilled crust mixture.

Bake on the hot sheet pan until some of the top crumbles are golden, about 35 minutes. Transfer the pan to a wire rack and let cool completely.

Using the parchment overhang as handles, lift the cooled square onto a cutting board. Cut into 16 square bars. Enjoy at room temperature or refrigerate and serve chilled. ●

MAKES 16 BARS

Crust

1½ cups (187 g) all-purpose flour

1 stick (113 g) cold unsalted butter, cubed

1 large egg yolk

½ cup (100 g) granulated sugar

½ teaspoon baking powder

¼ teaspoon kosher salt

Strawberry Rambutan Filling

16 fresh rambutans, diced, or one 20 oz. (565 g) can rambutans drained and coarsely chopped (see Notes)

5½ oz. (160 g) diced strawberries (about 1 cup)

¼ cup (50 g) granulated sugar

1 tablespoon (8 g) cornstarch

Grated zest of 1 lemon

1 tablespoon (15 g) fresh lemon juice

⅛ teaspoon kosher salt

Notes: To pit fresh rambutans, slice a cheek on each side of the seed (like you would with a mango) and cut excess flesh from the top and bottom of the seed. This leaves behind a little cube with the seed inside, which you'll discard.

Canned rambutans, even after you drain them, have a significant amount of liquid. So after you dice the fruit, pat it a couple times with a paper towel to sop up excess moisture.

Bukayo Macaroons

Farming was my grandparents' business. Every morning, my Lolo and Lola would pack up their harvest and sell the day's goods at the local palengke, or wet market. This was the bulk of how they made their living. But it wasn't the only avenue for profit. While my grandparents faced the bustle of retail, my Uncle George, the oldest of eleven children, would boil batches of bukayo, flat and crispy coconut sweets, reminiscent of macaroons. My mom and her sisters would package them in plastic—twelve discs in each clear bag. Most were sold wholesale to sari-saris (neighborhood convenience stores), where kids could buy them individually. But some were sold on foot, peddler-style. My uncle's bukayo was very popular, and sometimes villagers would even come to the house to purchase a small parcel, adding a few ripe guavas or a stalk of sugarcane to their tab while they were there.

My family's recipe uses fresh coconut grated into long noodles. But I blitz mine in a food processor just to make life a little easier. Brown sugar adds a warm caramel flavor, and a garnish of melted chocolate adds a fudgy, bitter note. But the ticket is a frothy egg white folded into the mixture, which lifts the normally compact texture into crisp and chewy macaroon territory.

In a large nonstick skillet, bring ½ cup (120 g) of the coconut water to a steady simmer over medium-high heat. Immediately stir in the coconut and cook until the water has evaporated, about 2 minutes.

Reduce to a gentle simmer over medium-low heat. Stir in the remaining ¼ cup (60 g) of coconut water, the brown sugar, and salt. Cook, occasionally stirring and spreading into an even layer, until nearly all the moisture has evaporated and the coconut is tender, glossy, and even a little translucent (like caramelized onions), about 15 minutes.

Transfer to a large bowl and let cool to room temperature, about 30 minutes.

Meanwhile, preheat the oven to 350°F (180°C). Line two sheet pans with parchment paper.

In a medium bowl, whisk the egg white vigorously by hand until foamy. Fold into the cooled coconut mixture.

Using a 1-tablespoon scoop, scoop mounds of the mixture onto the prepared sheet pans. Smooth down any flyaways. You can leave them as is for classic chewy macaroons or, for a crispier but still chewy cookie-shaped macaroon, flatten the mounds into 2-inch (5 cm) discs.

Bake one sheet pan at a time until the edges are golden, about 15 minutes. Transfer the pan to a wire rack and let cool for 5 minutes. Transfer the macaroons to the wire rack and let cool completely.

Place the macaroons on a parchment-lined baking sheet (you can use the same one you baked with as long as it's cool). Drizzle with melted chocolate and let set before serving. ●

MAKES 20 MACAROONS

¾ cup (180 g) coconut water or water, divided

2½ cups (225 g) coarsely grated fresh coconut (see Note)

¾ cup (150 g) dark brown sugar

⅛ teaspoon kosher salt

1 large egg white, at room temperature

Melted dark chocolate, for drizzling

Note: You'll need one fresh coconut but won't use all the meat. Scrape the meat and pulse a few times in a food processor until coarsely grated.

A family side hustle

Calamansi Coconut Bars

Calamansi, sometimes referred to as Philippine lime or Philippine lemon, has a startling sourness that demands your attention. It's extraordinarily tart, sharp and astringent. Even after it's sweetened with sugar and swirled with thick velvety coconut milk, you'll still taste (and feel) its presence in this recipe. Shredded coconut is stirred into the filling, but most of it floats to the surface, reconfiguring into a stratum of chewiness that contrasts the tender middle and crisp shortbread base. If you can't find calamansi juice, a mixture of fresh lemon and lime juice is the next best thing to deliver that potent citrusy punch.

For the crust: Preheat the oven to 350°F (180°C). Grease an 8-inch (20 cm) square cake pan with cooking spray and line with parchment paper so there is overhang on two sides.

In a food processor, add the flour, butter, sugar, and salt. Pulse until small dough crumbles form.

Scatter the mixture into the prepared pan and press firmly into the bottom.

Bake until golden brown all over and deep golden around the perimeter, 30 to 35 minutes. Transfer the pan to a wire rack and let cool for 15 minutes. Leave the oven on.

For the filling: In a large bowl, beat the eggs with a whisk. Whisk in the sugar, coconut milk, calamansi juice, coconut extract, and salt. Whisk in the flour and baking powder. Stir in 1 cup (50 g) of the coconut with a fork.

Pour the filling over the cooled crust and sprinkle with the remaining ¼ cup (12 g) of coconut.

Bake until set and golden around the perimeter, 30 to 35 minutes. Transfer the pan to a wire rack and let cool completely. Cover with foil and refrigerate until chilled, at least 3 hours.

Using the parchment overhang as handles, lift the chilled square onto a cutting board. Cut into 16 square bars. Enjoy chilled or at room temperature. ●

MAKES 16 BARS

Crust

1 cup (125 g) all-purpose flour

1 stick (113 g) cold unsalted butter, cubed

⅓ cup (66 g) granulated sugar

⅛ teaspoon kosher salt

Filling and Topping

4 large eggs, at room temperature

¾ cup (175 g) granulated sugar

¼ cup (60 g) canned unsweetened coconut milk

¼ cup (60 g) calamansi juice

¼ teaspoon coconut extract

¼ teaspoon kosher salt

¼ cup (31 g) all-purpose flour

1 teaspoon baking powder

1¼ cups (62 g) unsweetened shredded coconut, divided

Mochi-Stuffed Chocolate Chip Cookies

I love a gooey, chewy chocolate chip cookie. And these are probably the gooiest, chewiest cookies I've ever had. Tucked inside
each one is a soft and squishy cushion of mochi that, when eaten
warm, is stretchy and melty. Mochi, with its glutinous texture and
fragrant rice flavor, was a popular after-school snack for me, especially when I was living in Japan. If you're worried that mochi is too
much of a challenge to make, don't be. This one takes shape in the
microwave and it's pretty difficult to mess up. In order to divide
the mochi into perfectly even portions, I do recommend a scale
(which as you may know by now, I prefer to use for every recipe).

For the chocolate chip cookies: In a medium bowl, whisk together the flour,
baking powder, and baking soda.

To the bowl of a stand mixer fitted with the paddle, add the butter, brown
sugar, granulated sugar, and salt and beat on medium-high speed until pale
and fluffy, about 5 minutes. Beat in the egg and vanilla until combined.

With the mixer on the lowest speed setting, gradually add the flour mixture
and mix until almost combined but not quite. Add the chocolate and mix
until just combined.

Transfer the dough to a medium bowl. Cover with plastic wrap and refrigerate for at least 2 hours and up to overnight.

Using a 1-tablespoon scoop, scoop 34 mounds of the cookie dough (about
20 g each) onto a parchment-lined sheet pan.

Flatten each mound into a 2-inch (5 cm) disc (the pan will be crowded but
the spacing isn't important yet). Keep extra flour nearby in case things get
sticky. Refrigerate while you prepare the mochi.

For the mochi filling: Using a fine-mesh sieve, dust a little cornstarch over a
dinner plate.

In a medium microwave-safe bowl, whisk together the glutinous rice flour
and sugar. Add the water and whisk until there are no lumps. Cover the
bowl with a microwave-safe plate. Microwave for 30 seconds. The mixture
should start looking thicker and stickier. Stir well with a silicone spatula.
Continue to microwave in 30-second increments, stirring in between, until
the dough is gelatinous and holds its shape, another 1 to 2 minutes (this will
depend on the strength of your microwave).

Transfer the mochi to the prepared plate and dust the top with more cornstarch. Flatten slightly and let cool for 10 minutes.

Using kitchen shears and a digital scale, cut the mochi into 17 equal portions
(about 10 g each). Pinch and roll each portion into a small ball.

(Recipe continued on the following page).

MAKES 17 COOKIES

Chocolate Chip Cookies

1¾ cups (219 g) all-purpose
flour, plus extra for dusting

¾ teaspoon baking powder

¾ teaspoon baking soda

1 stick (113 g) unsalted butter,
at room temperature

¾ cup (150 g) dark brown
sugar

¼ cup (50 g) granulated sugar

1 teaspoon kosher salt

1 large egg, at room temperature

1 teaspoon vanilla extract

One 3.5 oz. (100 g) bar dark
chocolate (70% cacao),
chopped (about ⅔ cup)

Flaky sea salt, for sprinkling

Mochi Filling

Cornstarch, for dusting

½ cup plus 1 tablespoon (70 g)
glutinous rice flour

2 tablespoons (25 g) granulated sugar

½ cup (120 g) water

(Mochi-stuffed Chocolate Chip Cookies continued from previous page).

To assemble: Place a ball of mochi onto the center of 17 of the cookie dough discs. Sandwich with another disc, sealing the edges and rolling between your hands into a round ball (flour your hands lightly if the dough is sticking). Transfer the balls to a dinner plate (this will take up less space in the refrigerator) and chill until firm, 15 minutes.

Meanwhile, preheat the oven to 350°F (180°C).

Transfer 6 balls to a parchment-lined sheet pan (arranging in three rows of 2) and bake until puffed and spread, about 15 minutes. Transfer the pan to a wire rack. There will be a little lump in the middle of each cookie. Gently press it down with a spatula and sprinkle with flaky sea salt. Let cool for 5 minutes.

Repeat with the remaining dough, using a fresh parchment-lined sheet pan. These are best enjoyed while still warm.

Refrigerate in an airtight container. You can eat them as is, but I recommend reheating them in the microwave for 5 to 10 seconds to soften the mochi. The assembled dough freezes really well. If baking from frozen, bake for an extra 3 to 5 minutes. ●

Chewy Caramel Ampaw

Ampaw, also known as pop rice or puffed rice, is a crunchy dessert from the Cebu province in the Visayas region. Think of them like crispy rice treats, but denser and without the chewy marshmallow. Instead, they're coated in a golden caramel syrup and shaped into small spheres or bars.

Traditionally, ampaw is made by drying cooked rice under the hot sun and frying the grains until they're puffed and crisp. The obvious shortcut would be to just go out and buy puffed rice. But this defeats the pantry purge appeal. Luckily, the heart of this dish is also the heart of my pantry—rice. And making puffed rice from uncooked rice is surprisingly easy, not to mention fascinating.

This makes a great base for mixing in forgotten oddments lurking in your cupboard (e.g., cereal, chocolate chips, flaxseeds, unpurposed sprinkles). My version is noticeably softer than the original (I like it that way) and includes almonds, sunflower seeds, coconut flakes, and a finish of melted dark chocolate.

In the bowl of a rice cooker, add the rice and enough water to cover. Swish your hand around until the water turns a milky, cloudy white. Drain through a sieve. Repeat two more times.

Return the rice to the rice cooker bowl and add the ½ cup (120 g) of water (the water should no longer be cloudy). Place the bowl inside the rice cooker and turn it on to cook.

When the rice is finished cooking, scoop it out onto a parchment-lined sheet pan. Spread into an even layer using two forks to move around and de-clump the rice. You can also spray your hands with a little cooking spray and use your fingers. If you do this well, the rice will essentially be cold by the time you're finished (that's what you want).

Preheat the oven to 200°F (90°C).

Bake until the rice is dried and translucent, about 3 hours. (It won't be the same dryness as uncooked rice). Transfer the pan to a wire rack and let cool completely.

Line a sheet pan with paper towels and set it beside the stovetop. Attach a candy or digital probe thermometer to a heavy pot or Dutch oven and fill with 1 ½ inches (4 cm) of oil. Heat the oil to 375°F (190°C).

Dip a large fine-mesh sieve into the oil (like you're making a DIY French fry basket) and add half of the rice. Fry until puffed, stirring with a metal spoon, about 10 seconds. Lift the sieve and let it drain. Transfer the puffed rice to the lined sheet pan. Repeat with the remaining rice. You should have about 1 ¾ cups (400 ml) of puffed rice.

Line the bottom and sides of an 8-inch (20 cm) square cake pan with foil and spray with cooking spray.

In a large bowl, toss together the puffed rice, almonds, coconut, and sunflower seeds.

(Recipe continued on the following page).

MAKES 16 BARS

½ cup (105 g) medium-grain white rice, such as Botan Calrose (see Note)

½ cup (120 g) water , plus extra for rinsing the rice

Neutral oil, for deep-frying

½ cup (70 g) almonds, toasted and coarsely chopped

½ cup (30 g) unsweetened coconut flakes

2 tablespoons (15 g) sunflower seeds

6 tablespoons (114 g) light corn syrup

6 tablespoons (75 g) light brown sugar

⅛ teaspoon kosher salt

3 tablespoons (42 g) unsalted butter

¾ teaspoon vanilla bean paste or extract

Optional Garnishes flaky sea salt, melted dark chocolate, sprinkles

Note: You cannot used leftover cooked rice since it doesn't have as much moisture and will not fry up as puffy.

(Chewy Caramel Ampaw continued from previous page).

To a medium bowl, add the corn syrup, brown sugar, and salt.

In a small saucepan, heat the butter over medium heat, stirring occasionally, until melted and it turns toasty and brown, about 3 minutes. Remove from the heat and stir in the corn syrup and brown sugar mixture.

Return to the stovetop and cook over medium heat until the sugar is melted and it's bubbling nicely, about 2 minutes. Aim for 200° to 210°F (93° to 99°C) on an instant-read thermometer. Remove from the heat and stir in the vanilla.

Pour the warm syrup over the puffed rice mixture. Stir thoroughly with a rubber spatula until well combined. Transfer the mixture to the prepared pan. Spread and press firmly into an even layer, packing tightly.

Let cool completely for 20 minutes. Using the foil as handles, lift the bar onto a cutting board. Cut into 16 square bars. If you want, you can shape some of the squares into balls (that's how my mom likes them).

If you'd like to top with any extra garnishes, do that now while it's still a little sticky. Let the bars continue to cool for another 20 minutes to allow the caramel to stiffen up a bit. ●

03

Pies, Tarts & Crisps

Malted Lemon Egg Pie

When I was in high school, I worked at a classic American diner. The kind that serves burgers and hot dogs and fills Styrofoam cups with "good ice" (the soft pebbly kind) and frothy fountain sodas. Vintage homecoming photos and faded cheerleading uniforms decorated the walls. And we played the same CD of beach music every day, starting with "Build Me Up Buttercup." It was the first time I had ever used malted milk powder as an ingredient and I've never gone back. Just like it did for the shakes I made at sixteen, it gives this custardy egg pie that special something.

Filipino egg pies have a beguiling look about them, owing to a sepia-colored blanket of scorched meringue on their surface. When you fold the whipped egg white into the filling mixture, it doesn't meld into one. Instead, you're simply breaking up the meringue into hundreds of tiny bubbles, which swim upward and reorganize into a stratum of foam where they await the blazing touch of heat. My recipe calls on lemon juice and zest for a sunny pop of freshness. As for the malted milk powder, it lends a rich and roasty, sweet and savory quality. This soft custard pie tastes like a malted lemon milkshake. And you should make it. Don't break my heart.

For the pastry crust: In a food processor, add the flour, salt, and butter. Pulse until the butter is broken up into small bits. Add the water and pulse until the mixture looks like crumbled dough.

Transfer to an unfloured work surface. Gather and shape into a flat disc. Lightly dust the work surface with flour and roll out the dough into a 12-inch (30 cm) round.

Transfer to a 9-inch (23 cm) pie plate. There should be some overhanging dough. Tuck this excess under itself, all the way around, and pinch and shape into an evenly raised border, using the flat lip of the pie plate as a base. Flute or crimp the crust. Prick the dough all over with a fork. Refrigerate for at least 30 minutes and up to overnight.

Preheat the oven to 350°F (180°C). Set the pie plate on a sheet pan and line the pastry with foil so it covers the dough entirely. Fill with dried beans or pie weights.

Bake until the dough starts to look dry with a matte finish, 35 to 40 minutes. Remove the foil and beans and continue to bake (on the sheet pan) until the crust perimeter is light golden, 15 to 20 minutes.

Note: After you remove the foil and beans and return the pastry to the oven, it should not balloon in the center. If it does, put the foil and beans back and bake for another 5 to 10 minutes before continuing.

Transfer the pie plate to a wire rack and let cool while you make the filling. Reduce the oven temperature to 325°F (160°C).

For the filling: In a large bowl, combine the sugar and lemon zest and rub together with your fingers until moist and fragrant. Stir in the malted milk powder. Whisk in the evaporated milk, whole eggs, vanilla, and salt. Whisk in the lemon juice.

(Recipe continued on the following page).

MAKES ONE 9-INCH (23 CM) PIE

Pastry Crust

1⅓ cups plus 1 tablespoon (174 g) all-purpose flour, plus extra for dusting

¼ teaspoon kosher salt

6 tablespoons (85 g) cold unsalted butter, cubed

4 tablespoons (60 g) ice water

Filling

1 cup (200 g) granulated sugar

Grated zest of 4 lemons

2 tablespoons (14 g) malted milk powder

One 12 fl. oz. (354 ml) can evaporated milk

4 large eggs

1 tablespoon vanilla bean paste or extract

½ teaspoon kosher salt

2 tablespoons (30 g) fresh lemon juice

1 large egg white

(Malted Lemon Egg Pie continued from previous page).

In a medium bowl, using a hand mixer, beat the egg white on medium speed until soft peaks form (peaks are whipped and foamy but do not stand straight up), about 90 seconds.

Add the meringue to the milk mixture and stir with a rubber spatula until the meringue is sufficiently broken up and floats to the top, creating an even, foamy layer.

To assemble: Return the pie plate to the sheet pan and pour the filling into the crust. Bake until the top is golden, the edges are set, but the center jiggles slightly, 50 to 60 minutes. (The filling will puff up and shouldn't look liquidy).

Remove the pie (with the sheet pan) from the oven. If the top isn't sufficiently golden, preheat the broiler (choose high if it's an option and leave the rack in the center).

When the broiler is nice and hot, return the pie (on the sheet pan) to the oven. Broil until the meringue is deeply golden, about 2 minutes (this will depend on the strength of your broiler). Move the sheet pan around as needed to toast evenly.

Transfer the pie plate to a wire rack and let cool completely. Enjoy at room temperature or refrigerate and serve chilled. ●

Buko Cherry Crumble Pie

In the 1960s, a young woman named Soledad Pahud left the US and returned to her hometown, Laguna, with the goal of opening a bake-shop. She attempted to re-create the American apple pie, which she learned to make during her time abroad, but to no avail. Apples, not native to the Philippines, were hard to come by. Pahud, with the help of her sisters, turned to buko, young coconut, which flourishes across the islands. Destined to become a household name, buko pie was born.

Young coconuts aren't fully ripened and eventually mature into the brown hairy ones. Their skin is smooth and green and their meat is juicy, soft, and supple, even gelatinous at times. Tucked between two layers of buttery pie crust, buko creates a sumptuous and refreshing dessert very different from American coconut pies, which rely on dried coconut shreds or flakes.

Parts of Pahud's story may come down to local lore, but no one would contest that Laguna is home to the best buko pies in the land. What began as a family project turned into a family business and Pahud's bakery, The Orient, continues to draw hundreds of customers daily who hope to get their hands on "the original buko pie." The province is now home to many shops and hawkers dishing out the creamy pastry. There is no shortage of variety when it comes to buko pie, which has been remixed with the addition of lychee, pineapple, durian, and more.

My version paints the flaky bottom crust with a coat of cherry jam, giving each bite a snap of fruity tartness, while a crunchy cinnamon-kissed crumble sits on top like a bronze crown. This is very delicious.

For the buko filling: In a small saucepan, whisk together the coconut water and cornstarch. Whisk in the coconut milk, granulated sugar, malted milk powder, and salt. Cook over medium heat, whisking constantly, until bubbles are bursting on the surface and the mixture is thick like pudding, 3 to 5 minutes. Remove from the heat and whisk in the butter and vanilla.

Scrape the pudding into a large bowl and stir in the coconut meat with a dinner fork. Cover with plastic wrap so it touches the surface of the filling directly (this will prevent a skin from forming). Refrigerate until chilled, about 2 hours.

For the crumble topping: In a large bowl, whisk together the flour, brown sugar, cinnamon, and salt. Add the butter and toss to coat. Using your hands, rub the butter into the flour mixture until combined and doughy crumbles form. Set aside in the freezer.

For the pastry crust: In a food processor, add the flour, salt, and butter and pulse until the butter is broken up into small bits. Add the water and pulse until the mixture looks like crumbled dough.

Transfer to an unfloured work surface. Gather and shape into a flat disc. Lightly dust the work surface with flour and roll out the dough into a 12-inch (30.5 cm) round.

Transfer to a 9-inch (23 cm) pie plate. There should be some overhanging dough. Tuck this excess under itself, all the way around, and pinch and

MAKES ONE 9-INCH (23 CM) PIE

Filling

¾ cup (180 g) coconut water

¼ cup (33 g) cornstarch

¾ cup (180 g) canned unsweet-ened coconut milk

½ cup (100 g) granulated sugar

1 tablespoon (7 g) malted milk powder

½ teaspoon kosher salt

1 tablespoon (14 g) unsalted butter

2 teaspoons vanilla bean paste or extract

13 oz. (375 g) coarsely chopped young coconut meat (about 2 ½ cups; see Note)

½ cup (156 g) cherry preserves, for assembly

Crumble Topping

1 cup (125 g) all-purpose flour

¼ cup (50 g) dark brown sugar

¼ teaspoon ground cinnamon

⅛ teaspoon kosher salt

1 stick (113 g) cold unsalted butter, cubed

Pastry Crust

1⅓ cups plus 1 tablespoon (174 g) all-purpose flour, plus extra for dusting

¼ teaspoon kosher salt

6 tablespoons (85 g) cold unsalted butter, cubed

4 tablespoons (60 g) ice water

Note: You'll need 4 young coconuts (I prefer the ivory ones with the pointed tops that have already been shaved), about 2 lbs (910 g) each. You can also use frozen young coconut meat, sold in Asian supermarkets, but I really do think fresh is a million times better.

shape into an evenly raised border, using the flat lip of the pie plate as a base. Flute or crimp the crust. Prick the dough all over with a fork. Refrigerate for at least 30 minutes and up to overnight.

Preheat the oven to 350°F (180°C). Set the pie plate on a sheet pan and line the pastry with foil so it covers the dough entirely. Fill with dried beans or pie weights.

Bake until the dough starts to look dry with a matte finish around the inside perimeter, 25 to 30 minutes. Remove the foil and beans and continue to bake (still on the sheet pan) until the perimeter is light golden, 15 to 20 minutes.

Note: After you remove the foil and beans and return the pastry to the oven, it should not balloon in the center. If it does, put the foil and beans back and bake for another 5 to 10 minutes before continuing.

Transfer the pie plate to a wire rack and let cool for 15 minutes. Leave the oven on.

To assemble: Return the pie plate to the sheet pan and spread the cherry preserves over the bottom of the cooled pastry. Spoon dollops of the chilled buko filling over the jam (this makes it easier to spread while keeping the jam in place). Spread into an even layer and sprinkle with the frozen crumble topping.

Return to the oven and bake until the crust perimeter and parts of the crumb topping are golden brown, about 1 hour.

Transfer the pie plate to a wire rack and let cool for at least 1 hour. Enjoy slightly warm, at room temperature, or chilled. ●

Bourbon Brown Butter Cashew Tart

The Philippines meets the American South in this recipe, where cashew boat tarts (named for their tiny ship shape) embrace the appearance of bourbon pecan pie. Nutty and rich with caramel, I could easily throw back three or four boat tarts in one sitting as a kid. This is probably the equivalent of a slice of pie, which is, apparently, what I was really after. Here, browned butter deepens all the flavors at play, while sticky golden syrup adds a luscious buttery sweetness unmatched by honey or corn syrup. If you can't find it at your local market (it's a British import), it's definitely worth seeking out via the Internet. Taking the caramel up to 235°F (113°C), a temperature mark titled "softball stage" in candy making, ensures a firm chewy filling. But the star here is truly the cashews, which lend a soft crunchy bite.

For the pastry crust: In a food processor, add the flour, salt, and butter and pulse until the butter is broken up into small bits. Add the water and pulse until the mixture looks like crumbled dough.

Transfer to an unfloured work surface. Gather and shape into a flat disc. Lightly dust the work surface with flour and roll out the dough into a 12-inch (30.5 cm) round.

Transfer to a 9-inch (23 cm) tart tin with a removable bottom. Roll a rolling pin over the dough to trim away the excess and create clean edges. Prick the dough all over with a fork. Refrigerate for at least 30 minutes and up to overnight.

Preheat the oven to 350°F (180°C). Set the tart tin on a sheet pan and line the pastry with foil so it covers the dough entirely. Fill with dried beans or pie weights.

Bake until the dough starts to look dry with a matte finish around the inner perimeter, 25 to 30 minutes. Remove the foil and beans and continue to bake (on the sheet pan) until the crust perimeter is light golden, 15 to 20 minutes.

Note: After you remove the foil and beans and return the pastry to the oven, it should not balloon in the center. If it does, put the foil and beans back and bake for another 5 to 10 minutes before continuing.

Transfer the tart tin (on the sheet pan) to a wire rack and let cool for 15 minutes. Leave the oven on.

For the filling: Meanwhile, in a medium bowl, beat the eggs with a whisk. Set beside the stovetop.

In a large saucepan, heat the butter over medium heat, stirring occasionally, until melted and it turns toasty and brown, about 5 minutes. Transfer to a small bowl.

In the same large saucepan, whisk together the brown sugar, golden syrup, heavy cream, and salt. Have an instant-read thermometer ready. Bring to a boil over high heat. Boil, whisking constantly, until the thermometer registers 235°F (113°C), about 1 minute (this can happen fast).

MAKES ONE 9-INCH (23 CM) TART

Pastry Crust

1⅓ cups plus 1 tablespoon (174 g) all-purpose flour, plus extra for dusting

¼ teaspoon kosher salt

6 tablespoons (85 g) cold unsalted butter, cubed

4 tablespoons (60 g) ice water

Filling

2 large eggs, at room temperature

4 tablespoons (56 g) unsalted butter

½ cup (100 g) light brown sugar

½ cup plus 1 tablespoon (169 g) golden syrup

2 tablespoons (30 g) heavy cream

⅛ teaspoon kosher salt

1 tablespoon (15 g) bourbon

2 teaspoons vanilla extract

1½ cups (210 g) lightly salted roasted cashews, coarsely chopped

The Philippines meets the American South

Remove from the heat and whisk in the brown butter, bourbon, and vanilla.

Gradually whisk about half of the warm syrup mixture into the eggs. Then whisk the egg mixture back into the saucepan.

To assemble the pie: Spread the cashews over the bottom of the cooled crust and pour the syrup mixture over top.

Return to the oven and bake until the filling is puffed (it will settle as it cools) and set, about 30 minutes.

Transfer the tart tin to a wire rack and let cool for at least 20 minutes. Serve slightly warm or at room temperature. ●

Pineapple Pie

I peel pineapple the same way my mom (and probably every other Filipino mom) does: carved into the shape of a fusilli noodle, the eyes whittled away in a diagonal spiral leaving rippled ravines in the fruit's golden flesh. Pineapple pie is a Philippine bakeshop specialty. The crust is a little breadier than your typical pie crust, owing to yeast or, in this case, baking powder. My trick to ensure an extra crispy, sturdy crust is to preheat a sheet pan on the lowest oven rack for 30 minutes. This is essentially a DIY pizza stone. Scorching the bottom crust right away is vital because there is a *lot* of custardy filling on top and this isn't the kind of pie you can blind bake.

If you love pineapple as much as I do, you'll be tempted to eat the filling straight up. It's sweet, fruity, and refreshing, and I've found that a bit of orange zest amplifies its brilliant citrusy profile. A generous shower of turbinado sugar is sprinkled on top before it bakes, which adds a satisfying crunch and a gorgeous glimmer (a simple way to upgrade any pie or pastry, really). I skip the silverware and eat this the Filipino way, kamayan (by hand).

For the filling: In a medium bowl, add the egg yolks. Set beside the stovetop.

In a blender or food processor, puree the pineapple until smooth.

In a large saucepan, whisk together the water and cornstarch. Whisk in the pineapple puree, sugar, and salt. Heat over high heat, whisking constantly, until warm and steaming, about 2 minutes. Turn off the heat.

Gradually whisk about half of the warm pineapple mixture into the yolks. Then whisk the yolk mixture back into the saucepan. Cook over high heat, whisking constantly, until bubbles are bursting on the surface and the mixture is very thick and glazy (like a thick lemon curd), 3 to 5 minutes.

Remove from the heat and whisk in the butter, vanilla, and orange zest. Transfer the filling to a large bowl or liquid measuring cup. You should have about 4 cups (1200 g). Cover with plastic wrap and refrigerate until cold, at least 3 hours.

For the pastry crust: In a food processor, add the flour, salt, and baking powder and pulse to combine. Add the butter and shortening and pulse until they're broken up into small bits. Add the heavy cream and pulse to distribute. Add the water and pulse until the mixture looks like crumbled dough.

Transfer the dough to an unfloured work surface. Gather into a uniform mass. Divide the dough into 2 equal portions (about 460 g each) and shape each into a flat disc. Wrap each disc in plastic wrap and refrigerate for 1 hour.

To assemble: Lightly dust a work surface with flour and roll out one disc of dough into a 15 × 12-inch (38 × 30 cm) rectangle.

Transfer the dough to a quarter-sheet pan, letting the excess dough hang over all sides. Add the chilled filling and spread into an even layer.

(Recipe continued on the following page).

MAKES 16 SLICES

Filling

4 large egg yolks

25 oz. (715 g) fresh pineapple, cubed

½ cup (120 g) water

½ cup (66 g) cornstarch

2 cups (400 g) granulated sugar

1 teaspoon kosher salt

2 tablespoons (28 g) unsalted butter

½ teaspoon vanilla bean paste or extract

Grated zest of 1 orange

Pastry Crust

4 cups (500 g) all-purpose flour, plus extra for dusting

2 teaspoons kosher salt

1½ teaspoons baking powder

1 stick (113 g) cold unsalted butter, cubed

6 tablespoons (60 g) vegetable shortening, cold

½ cup (120 g) heavy cream, cold

½ cup (120 g) ice water

1 large egg beaten with 1 tablespoon water, for egg wash

Turbinado sugar, for sprinkling

Special Equipment

One quarter-sheet pan (13 × 9-inch /33 × 23 cm)

A Philippine bakeshop specialty

(Pineapple Pie continued from previous page).

Roll out the second disc of dough into a 15 × 12-inch (38 × 30 cm) rectangle. Place the dough over the pineapple filling. (Try to get the placement correct the first time! The dough will stick to the filling, so it's hard to adjust once it's on there).

Pinch together the overhanging dough and tuck under itself like you would for a regular double-crusted pie. Shape into a neat crust (this will be fairly tall and thick). Using kitchen shears, trim slivers of dough off the top of the crust and reshape until you have a thick (but not too thick) crust all the way around.

Brush the dough all over with the egg wash and poke all over with a fork (make sure there are actual holes not just imprints). Sprinkle with turbinado sugar. Freeze for 15 minutes. Then refrigerate for 15 minutes.

Meanwhile, place a foil-lined standard half-sheet pan on the lowest oven rack position and preheat to 350°F (180°C) for 30 minutes.

Place the pineapple pie on the hot sheet pan and bake until the crust is golden brown, about 1 hour.

Transfer the pie (still on the sheet pan) to a wire rack. Don't worry if the pie is leaking in a few spots. If the pastry looks slightly raised, gently press it down with a rubber spatula to expel any air. Let cool for 1 hour.

Invert the pie onto a wire rack. Then invert again onto another wire rack so it sits right side up. Let cool completely, about 1 ½ hours.

Slide the pie onto a cutting board. Using a serrated knife, cut the pie into 4 equal rectangles. Cut each rectangle in half vertically into smaller rectangles (not super skinny ones). You should have 8 equal rectangles. Cut each rectangle diagonally into 2 triangles.

Enjoy at room temperature or refrigerate and serve chilled (which I like better). ●

Fruit Salad Pie

In the first month of working on this cookbook, my mom called to remind me not to forget fruit salad. As if I would. Fruit salad made a regular appearance in my household growing up, not least because it requires no actual cooking or even a knife. All of the fruit, which is canned, is simply tossed with sweetened condensed milk and folded with Cool Whip. My version reconfigures what is essentially a fruit-and-cream salad into a fruit-and-cream pie, set within a crispy honey graham cracker crust. Cold cream is whipped to lofty stiff peaks, fortified with gelatin, and sweetened with a thick, generous stream of sticky condensed milk.

I prefer using a blend of canned and fresh fruit. The only caveat is that many fresh tropical fruits (such as pineapple, mango, and kiwi) have enzymes that prevent gelatin from setting properly. It's possible to denature these enzymes by cooking them first. But that's too much work in my opinion. Fortunately, all canned fruits are actually cooked. Problem solved. Everything else, from berries to stone fruits, is pretty much fair game.

Preheat the oven to 350°F (180°C). Lightly grease a 9-inch (23 cm) pie plate with cooking spray.

In a large bowl, stir together the graham cracker crumbs, sugar, and salt. Add the melted butter and stir with a fork, mashing the butter into the mixture, until well combined. It should be wet, sandy, and hold together when squished by hand.

Press firmly into the bottom and sides of the prepared pie plate. (The bottom of a small dry measuring cup helps with this).

Bake until set and light golden, about 10 minutes. Transfer the pie plate to a wire rack and immediately press gently again with the bottom of a measuring cup. Let cool completely.

Drain the canned fruit and spread out on a paper towel–lined plate. Pat dry with more paper towels to remove as much moisture as possible. Do a good job of this.

Pour the water into a small microwave-safe bowl and sprinkle the gelatin evenly over top. Whisk together and let absorb for 5 minutes. Microwave until melted, about 10 seconds. Whisk in 2 teaspoons (10 g) of the heavy cream.

In a large bowl, using a hand mixer, beat the remaining 1 cup (240 g) of the heavy cream on medium-high speed until soft peaks form, about 2 minutes. With the mixer running, slowly drizzle in the gelatin mixture and beat until combined and stiff peaks form, about 30 seconds.

Add the sweetened condensed milk all at once and beat on low speed until fluffy and combined, about 30 seconds. Fold in the canned and fresh fruit.

Transfer the filling to the cooled crust and spread it out, swooping and swirling to create a pretty textured surface. Refrigerate until set, at least 3 hours, but overnight is best. ●

MAKES ONE 9-INCH (23 CM) PIE

1¾ cups (175 g) finely ground graham cracker crumbs

¼ cup (50 g) granulated sugar

⅛ teaspoon kosher salt

1 stick (113 g) unsalted butter, melted

One 15 oz. (425 g) can fruit cocktail

¼ cup (60 g) water

One ¼ oz. (7 g) envelope unflavored gelatin powder

1 cup (240 g) plus 2 teaspoons (10 g) heavy cream, cold, divided

⅓ cup plus 2 tablespoons (147 g) sweetened condensed milk

1½ cups (8 oz./225 g) diced fresh fruit (such as strawberries, blackberries, peaches, or cherries)

Chocolate Meringue Boat Tarts

Boat tarts are named for their shape, which imply they're ready to voyage across the open seas. Cashew is certainly a classic choice (page 90), but they come in many different flavors and are often wrapped in colorful cellophane, just like polvoron. My boat tarts are filled with a dreamy chocolate ganache, enhanced with woody cinnamon, espresso, and sweet almond extract. Each one is topped with a trio of crisp meringue kisses, like the billowing sails on a ship. This is a project, to be sure, but it's actually lining the tiny tins with pastry that requires the most patience. That said, you'll be rewarded with striking and decadent tarts that, when displayed together, resemble a regal ocean fleet.

For the pastry crust: Cut 10 small rectangles of foil, about 5 × 3 inches (13 × 7.5 cm).

In a large bowl, whisk together the flour, powdered sugar, and salt. Add the butter, egg yolk, and water and beat with an electric hand mixer, breaking up the butter, until crumbly. Knead by hand, in the bowl, until the dough comes together. Divide into 10 equal portions (about 22 g each) and shape into oval logs.

Working with one portion at a time, dip the bottom of a log in flour and place in a boat tart tin. Press into an even layer. Using your thumb to shape the dough, create a hollow in the center by pushing the dough into the bottom and up the sides. As the dough rises up the sides, scrape it off the rim to create clean edges.

Once all the tins are lined, prick the dough all over with a fork. Arrange the tins on a sheet pan. Line each pastry tart with a square of foil, pressing into the crevices, so it covers the dough entirely. Fill with dried beans or pie weights. Refrigerate for at least 30 minutes.

Meanwhile, preheat the oven to 350°F (180°C).

Bake until the dough starts to look dry with a matte finish, about 20 minutes. Remove the foil and beans and continue to bake until light golden all over, about 10 minutes.

Transfer the sheet pan to a wire rack and let cool for 10 minutes. Reduce the oven temperature to 225°F (110°C).

Remove the pastry shells from the tins and transfer them to the wire rack to cool completely.

For the meringue: Place an empty tart tin upside down on a sheet of parchment paper and trace the outline with pencil. Repeat until you've drawn 10 outlines, spaced evenly apart. Mark a small dot in the center of each outline. Flip the parchment paper over (so the pencil markings are on the bottom) onto a sheet pan.

To the bowl of a stand mixer fitted with the whisk, add the egg white and cream of tartar and beat on medium-high speed until foamy, 1 to 2 minutes. Slowly add the sugar (it takes about 2 minutes to add all the sugar). Turn off the mixer and scrape down the bowl. Beat on high speed until it's thick and sticky (like a marshmallow) and holds a strong peak with a little curl at the tip, 3 to 4 minutes.

MAKES 10 BOAT TARTS

Pastry Crust

1 cup (125 g) all-purpose flour

2 tablespoons (12 g) powdered sugar

¼ teaspoon kosher salt

4 tablespoons (56 g) unsalted butter, at room temperature

1 large egg yolk

1 tablespoon (15 g) water

Meringue

1 large egg white, at room temperature

⅛ teaspoon cream of tartar

¼ cup (50 g) granulated sugar

Ganache

3 oz. (85 g) dark chocolate (70% cacao), chopped

1½ tablespoons (18 g) granulated sugar

¼ teaspoon ground cinnamon

⅛ teaspoon instant coffee or espresso powder

⅛ teaspoon kosher salt

3 tablespoons (45 g) boiling water

¼ teaspoon almond extract

Special Equipment

Ten 9.5 × 4 × 1.5 cm boat tart tins (see Note)

Note: Boat tart tins are widely available on Amazon.

Transfer the meringue to a pastry bag fitted with a large French star tip (Wilton #8B or Ateco 869).

To keep the parchment paper in place, pipe a small dot of meringue onto the four corners of the sheet pan and press the parchment corners onto it so it sticks.

Working with one traced outline at a time, pipe a mound of meringue on the center dot. Pipe a slightly shorter mound on each side so they're touching the center mound. A 3-inch (7.5 cm) row is ideal, but really just stay within the traced outline.

If you have leftover meringue after you've already piped 10 rows, pipe a few extra. It's good to have a few spares on hand.

Bake until the meringues are no longer sticky to the touch and are starting to develop a matte finish, about 45 minutes.

Turn off the oven and let the meringues dry out completely with the oven door closed, about 2 hours.

For the ganache: In a medium microwave-safe bowl, add the chocolate, sugar, cinnamon, instant coffee, and salt. Pour the boiling water over top and let sit for 5 minutes. Whisk until smooth. If it's not totally melted, microwave in 10-second increments, whisking after each. Whisk in the almond extract.

Dividing evenly, pour the ganache into the cooled pastry shells (about 14 g each). Tilt the tarts back and forth to distribute the ganache into an even layer. Let sit at room temperature until the ganache is set, about 1 hour.

Top each boat tart with a row of meringue, pressing gently to adhere.

Store at room temperature in an airtight container for 5 to 7 days. Don't be tempted to refrigerate them as it will cause the ganache to fully harden and the meringue to soften. ●

Boat tarts are named for their shape, which imply they're ready to voyage across the open seas.

Pandan Coconut Cream Pie

Coconut and pandan might as well be soulmates. They belong together. It's a partnership revered across Southeast Asia and one I re-create again and again throughout this book (Raspberry Buko Pandan Cake, page 24, and Southeast Tiramisu, page 142, for example). The long blade-shaped leaves of pandan, known as "vanilla of the East," wield an elusive flavor that's tropical, grassy, nutty, and sweet. When allied with coconut, so creamy and buttery, it creates a nearly perfect match. Here their exquisite flavors sing together without the distraction of anything else, save for a splash of lime juice to break through the richness. This pie is very coconutty and very pandan-y. It's sophisticated yet simple. And I mean that as a compliment.

For the pastry crust: In a food processor, add the flour, salt, and butter and pulse until the butter is broken up into small bits. Add the water and pulse until the mixture looks like crumbled dough.

Transfer to an unfloured work surface. Gather and shape into a flat disc. Lightly dust the work surface with flour and roll out the dough into a 12-inch (30 cm) round.

Transfer to a 9-inch (23 cm) pie plate. There should be some overhanging dough. Tuck this excess under itself, all the way around, and pinch and shape into an evenly raised border, using the flat lip of the pie plate as a base. Flute or crimp the crust. Prick the dough all over with a fork. Refrigerate for at least 30 minutes and up to overnight.

Preheat the oven to 350°F (180°C). Set the pie plate on a sheet pan and line the pastry with foil so it covers the dough entirely. Fill with dried beans or pie weights.

Bake until the dough starts to look dry with a matte finish, 35 to 40 minutes. Remove the foil and beans and continue to bake (on the sheet pan) until the crust is light golden all over, 20 to 25 minutes.

Note: After you remove the foil and beans and return the pastry to the oven, it should not balloon in the center. If it does, put the foil and beans back and bake for another 5 to 10 minutes before continuing.

Transfer the pie plate to a wire rack and let cool completely.

For the filling: In a small food processor, add the pandan leaves and water and puree. Scrape down the sides as needed and resist the urge to add more water. It won't look like it's blending well, but you just want to get the pandan really pulverized.

Place a fine-mesh sieve over a liquid measuring cup and strain the mixture, pressing with a rubber spatula to extract the green liquid. You should have ¼ cup (60 g) pandan juice (if you're short for whatever reason, just add a little water).

In a medium bowl, whisk together the pandan juice and cornstarch. Whisk in the egg yolks and set beside the stovetop.

In a large saucepan, whisk together the coconut milk, sugar, and salt. Heat over medium heat, whisking occasionally, until warm and steaming, about 5 minutes. Turn off the heat.

(Recipe continued on following page).

MAKES ONE 9-INCH (23 CM) PIE

Pastry Crust

1⅓ cups plus 1 tablespoon (174 g) all-purpose flour, plus extra for dusting

¼ teaspoon kosher salt

6 tablespoons (85 g) cold unsalted butter, cubed

4 tablespoons (60 g) ice water

Filling

8 frozen pandan leaves (about 65 g), cut into small pieces (see Note)

¼ cup (60 g) water

¼ cup (33 g) cornstarch

4 large egg yolks, at room temperature

One 13.5 fl. oz. (400 ml) can unsweetened coconut milk

½ cup (100 g) granulated sugar

¼ teaspoon kosher salt

1 cup (50 g) unsweetened shredded coconut

5 teaspoons (25 g) fresh lime juice

1 tablespoon (14 g) unsalted butter

¼ teaspoon coconut extract

Meringue Topping

2 large egg whites, at room temperature

¼ cup (50 g) granulated sugar

⅛ teaspoon cream of tartar

Pinch of kosher salt

Special Equipment

Kitchen torch

Note: In place of frozen pandan leaves, combine the ¼ cup (60 g) water with ⅛ teaspoon green pandan paste.

(Pandan Coconut Cream Pie continued from previous page).

Gradually whisk the warm coconut mixture into the pandan mixture. Pour it back into the saucepan and cook over medium heat, whisking constantly, until thick like pudding, about 2 minutes.

Remove from the heat and whisk in the shredded coconut, lime juice, butter, and coconut extract.

Scrape the filling into the cooled crust and spread into an even layer. Cover with plastic wrap so it touches the surface of the pudding (this will prevent a skin from forming). Refrigerate until chilled and set, at least 4 hours, but overnight is best.

For the meringue topping: Bring a pot of water to a simmer (your stand mixer bowl should be able to sit over the pot without the bottom of the bowl touching the water). Fit the stand mixer with the whisk.

In the stand mixer bowl, whisk together the egg whites, sugar, cream of tartar, and salt. Set the bowl over the pot of simmering water and cook, whisking constantly, until the sugar is dissolved and an instant-read thermometer registers 160°F (71°C), about 4 minutes.

Fasten the bowl into the stand mixer and beat on high speed until glossy stiff peaks form (peaks should stand straight up and not curl at the tip), about 2 minutes.

Transfer the meringue to a large pastry bag (see Note) fitted with a medium French star tip (Wilton #6B). Pipe dollops of the meringue around the perimeter of the filling. Repeat two more times so you have three concentric circles of meringue and a small bare round of pudding in the center.

Toast the meringue with a kitchen torch. Alternatively, use your oven broiler to toast the meringue (but watch it carefully). ●

Note: If you'd rather not pipe the meringue, simply spread over the top, swooping and swirling to create whimsical peaks.

Coconut and pandan might as well be soulmates.

They belong together.

Bubble Tea Tart

When I was working as a recipe developer for Food Network, I'd leave the kitchen early on summer Fridays. Once I made it back to my neighborhood, I'd detour for a bubble tea on West 72nd Street and walk my dog, Winnie, in the park while I sipped and pretended to listen to music on my headphones (sometimes I just want to enjoy my thoughts and the sounds of the city while discouraging random conversation). It was a way for me to decompress after the week, a simple pleasure. This cold and creamy custard tart, set inside a savory crust, is the perfect vehicle for bubble tea's luscious flavors. A couple of ingredients are deserving of recognition. The powdered milk heightens the milky flavor without adding any extra liquid to the filling. Instead of brown sugar, molasses (which makes brown sugar brown) is the key to creating the trendy Taiwanese tiger stripes on the surface of the custard. It imparts a deep flavor and a beautiful umber hue. You can prepare the tart ahead of time. Just be sure to hold off on making the boba until right before you serve, so it's at its chewiest.

For the pastry crust: In a food processor, add the flour, salt, and butter and pulse until the butter is broken up into small bits. Add the water and pulse until the mixture looks like crumbled dough.

Transfer to an unfloured work surface. Gather and shape into a flat disc. Lightly dust the work surface with flour and roll out the dough into a 12-inch (30 cm) round.

Transfer to a 9-inch (23 cm) tart tin with a removable bottom. Roll a rolling pin over the dough to trim away the excess and create clean edges. Prick the dough all over with a fork. Refrigerate for at least 30 minutes and up to overnight.

Preheat the oven to 350°F (180°C). Set the tart tin on a sheet pan and line the pastry with foil so it covers the dough entirely. Fill with dried beans or pie weights.

Bake until the dough starts to look dry with a matte finish, 35 to 40 minutes. Remove the foil and beans and continue to bake (on the sheet pan) until the pastry is light golden all over, 20 to 25 minutes.

Note: After you remove the foil and beans and return the pastry to the oven, it should not balloon in the center. If it does, put the foil and beans back and bake for another 5 to 10 minutes before continuing.

Transfer the tart tin to a wire rack and let cool for 15 minutes. Reduce the oven temperature to 325°F (160°C).

For the filling: In a medium bowl, beat the eggs with a whisk. Set beside the stovetop. Place a fine-mesh sieve over another medium bowl (you want this ready to go).

In a small saucepan, whisk together the heavy cream, milk, sugar, milk powder, and salt. Heat over medium heat until warm and steaming, about 3 minutes. Turn off the heat.

(Recipe continued on following page).

MAKES ONE 9-INCH (23 CM) TART

Pastry Crust

1⅓ cups plus 1 tablespoon (174 g) all-purpose flour, plus extra for dusting

¼ teaspoon kosher salt

6 tablespoons (85 g) cold unsalted butter, cubed

4 tablespoons (60 g) ice water

Filling

4 large eggs, at room temperature

¾ cup (180 g) heavy cream

¾ cup (180 g) whole milk

¼ cup (50 g) granulated sugar

2 tablespoons (10 g) nonfat dry milk powder

¼ teaspoon kosher salt

2 teaspoons vanilla extract

1½ teaspoons (11 g) molasses

Boba Topping

¼ cup (50 g) dark brown sugar

2 tablespoons (30 g) water

½ cup (80 g) black sugar boba pearls

(Bubble Tea Tart continued from previous page).

Gradually whisk the warm milk mixture into the eggs. Pour the mixture back into the saucepan. Cook over low heat, whisking constantly, until slightly thickened (like a pourable custard sauce), about 7 minutes. You want to heat this very, very slowly. Once you start to feel the mixture thicken, it's essentially done.

Immediately strain the mixture through the fine-mesh sieve (this will smooth it out). If the custard looks a little curdled (it happens), puree it in a food processor (or use an immersion blender) and strain once more. Whisk in the vanilla.

Transfer 1 tablespoon (15 g) of the custard to a pinch bowl and whisk in the molasses.

Pour the plain custard into the cooled crust. Using a spoon, drizzle the molasses custard on top of the plain custard in a stripey pattern (like you're drawing a bunch of wide flattened S shapes down the custard). Drag a chopstick through the drizzle (following the same S shape pattern as before) to create a stripey, softly swirled design.

Bake the tart (on the sheet pan) until about 1 inch (2.5 cm) of the filling perimeter is set, but the center still jiggles, 25 to 30 minutes.

Transfer the tart tin to a wire rack and let cool completely. Refrigerate until chilled and set, at least 3 hours.

For the boba topping: In a small saucepan, whisk together the brown sugar and water. Bring to a boil over high heat. Reduce to medium-low heat. Simmer, whisking occasionally, until slightly thickened, about 1 minute. Transfer to a medium heatproof bowl and let cool to room temperature (the syrup will thicken as it cools).

Meanwhile, prepare the boba according to the package directions. Cool the boba by rinsing with cold water and drain well. Stir the boba into the cooled brown sugar syrup.

If serving the whole tart (see Note), spoon the boba (draining off the excess syrup with a spoon) over the tart. This will carry some of the syrup to the tart but you don't want to add too much or you'll cover up the beautiful swirl design.

Note: Because boba has a tendency to harden up after a couple hours, this tart is best eaten immediately. If you don't plan on eating the whole tart at once, serve the tart in slices and top with the boba. Store the remaining boba pearls in the syrup in the refrigerator and gently reheat to soften the pearls as needed. ●

Cinnamon Chayote Crisp

My mom added chayote to brothy soups and stews when I was growing up. I don't remember particularly loving the vegetable (which is actually a fruit) as a child, or disliking it either, for that matter, but I've since recognized its virtues. It's crunchy and tender like a cucumber and adds bulk like zucchini or potatoes. It's basically flavorless, conceding to the essence of neighboring ingredients, meaning it has endless potential for interpretation. Here the bumpy-skinned squash coalesces with cinnamon and buttery brown sugar streusel in a sweet and humble crisp. Serve it with ice cream, a trickle of maple syrup, or simply on its own.

Preheat the oven to 350°F (180°C).

For the crisp topping: In a large bowl, whisk together the flour, oats, brown sugar, cinnamon, and salt. Add the butter and toss to coat. Using your hands, rub the butter into the flour mixture until combined and doughy crumbles form. Set aside in the freezer while you make the filling.

For the filling: In a 9-inch (23 cm) deep-dish pie plate, whisk together the brown sugar, flour, cinnamon, and salt. Add the chayote, lemon zest, and lemon juice and toss to combine.

Scatter the frozen crisp topping over the chayote mixture. Bake until the filling is bubbling and the crisp topping is light golden, about 1 hour.

Transfer the pie plate to a wire rack and let cool for at least 20 minutes. Enjoy warm or at room temperature. ●

MAKES ONE 9-INCH (23 CM) CRISP

Crisp Topping

1 cup (125 g) all-purpose flour

1 cup (100 g) old-fashioned oats

¼ cup (50 g) light brown sugar

¼ teaspoon ground cinnamon

⅛ teaspoon kosher salt

1 stick (113 g) cold unsalted butter, cubed

Filling

¼ cup (50 g) light brown sugar

1 tablespoon (8 g) all-purpose flour

½ teaspoon ground cinnamon

¼ teaspoon kosher salt

3 chayote squash (about 1½ lb. / 680 g), peeled, seeded, and diced small

Grated zest and juice of 1 large lemon

Sapin Sapin Cheesecake

I'm in the camp that believes cheesecake is another form of pie (yes, we exist). This one stacks ube shortbread with creamy coconut cheesecake and a sheet of radiant jackfruit gelatin. It's a tiered masterpiece inspired by the lateral stripes of sapin sapin, a chewy steamed cake made with glutinous rice flour and coconut milk, which translates to "layer by layer." I love how each bite transforms texturally, from crisp to creamy to jelly. And how it spans a range of flavors from earthy, to nutty, to bright. It's an experience. I like to top this with latik, crunchy pan-fried coconut curds, but toasted coconut flakes work just as well.

For the ube shortbread crust: Grease a 9-inch (23 cm) springform pan with cooking spray and line the bottom with parchment paper.

In a large bowl, using a hand mixer, beat together the butter, sugar, ube paste, and salt on medium speed until combined, about 15 seconds. Add the flour and beat on low speed until large dough crumbles form, about 1 minute.

Scatter the mixture evenly into the prepared pan and press firmly into the bottom. Freeze for 15 minutes.

Meanwhile, preheat the oven to 350°F (180°C).

Bake until dry and deep golden around the perimeter, 45 to 50 minutes. Transfer the pan to a wire rack and gently press the crust with the bottom of a small dry measuring cup. Let cool completely.

For the coconut cheesecake: In a large bowl, using a hand mixer, beat the heavy cream on medium-high speed until stiff peaks form, 2 to 3 minutes. Transfer to a small bowl and set aside in the refrigerator.

In the same large bowl (no need to clean), beat the cream cheese with the mixer on medium-high speed until very smooth. Add the powdered sugar, ⅔ cup (160 g) of the coconut cream, the coconut extract, vanilla, and salt. Beat on medium-high speed until just smooth and combined, about 30 seconds.

In a small microwave-safe bowl, add the water and sprinkle the gelatin evenly over top. Whisk and let absorb for 5 minutes. Microwave until melted, about 10 seconds.

Add the gelatin to the cream cheese mixture and beat on medium speed until combined, about 30 seconds. Fold in the whipped cream.

Spread the cheesecake filling evenly over the cooled ube crust. Cover with plastic wrap and refrigerate until set, about 2 hours.

For the latik curds: In a medium nonstick skillet, bring the remaining coconut cream to a boil over high heat. Reduce to a simmer over medium-low heat. Cook, stirring regularly with a silicone spatula, until the curds separate from the oil and become deep golden, 20 to 25 minutes. Adjust the heat as needed to maintain a simmer (not a boil).

Strain the latik through a fine-mesh sieve and let cool completely. Set aside in the refrigerator.

MAKES ONE 9-INCH (23 CM) CHEESECAKE

Ube Shortbread Crust

1½ sticks (170 g) unsalted butter, at room temperature

½ cup (100 g) granulated sugar

½ teaspoon ube paste

¼ teaspoon kosher salt

1½ cups (187 g) all-purpose flour

Coconut Cheesecake and Latik Curds

½ cup (120 g) heavy cream, cold

Two 8 oz. (226 g) packages cream cheese, at room temperature

1½ cups (150 g) powdered sugar

One 13.5 fl. oz. (400 ml) can coconut cream, divided

1½ teaspoons coconut extract

1 teaspoon vanilla bean paste or extract

¼ teaspoon kosher salt

¼ cup (60 g) water

2½ teaspoons (8 g) unflavored gelatin powder

Jackfruit Jelly

One 20 oz. (565 g) can jackfruit in syrup, drained and syrup reserved

1 tablespoon (15 g) fresh lemon juice

2 tablespoons (30 g) cold water

1½ teaspoons (5 g) unflavored gelatin powder

⅛ teaspoon kosher salt

For the jackfruit jelly: In a small food processor, add the jackfruit, 2 tablespoons (30 g) of the jackfruit syrup, and the lemon juice. Puree until as smooth as possible.

In a medium microwave-safe bowl, whisk together the water and another 2 tablespoons (30 g) of jackfruit syrup. Sprinkle the gelatin evenly over the top. Whisk together and let absorb for 5 minutes. Microwave until melted, about 10 seconds. Whisk in the jackfruit puree and salt.

Spread the mixture evenly over the cheesecake. Refrigerate until set, at least 1 hour.

Run a small offset spatula around the perimeter of the cheesecake to loosen the edges. Unlatch and remove the springform ring. Slide the cheesecake off of the springform base and onto a cake plate. If the parchment is still attached to the bottom, hold the cheesecake in place and pull away the parchment. Top with the latik curds. ●

Ube Macapuno Mont Blanc Tarts

I did a short *stage* at DANIEL on the Upper East Side. It was the only time I worked in a French brigade and I'll never forget it. Getting a taxi proved impossible the first day, so I ran all the way across the park, in a white chef's coat, lugging a five-pound knife bag over my shoulder. It was summer. I spent two hours picking microgreens, which I used to garnish every plate that evening. Once service began, the whole thing was like a dance. As I watched the last course go out, prepared attentively with dots and swirls, I didn't recognize much on the plate. It was the fanciest dessert I'd ever seen, in the fanciest restaurant I'd ever been in—a little tan crust topped with a little mountain of cocoa-colored frosting (my guess in the moment). I later discovered that this little treasure was a Mont Blanc. Sophisticated, elegant, completely cosmopolitan.

This fashionable sweet, named after the highest peak in the Alps, is classically made with a creamy chestnut puree piped into a pile of vermicelli. I love how it feigns fancy because in reality you can be a little messy about it and still end up with a very dramatic presentation. Beyond France and Italy, the Mont Blanc has amassed a devoted following in China and Japan, where a broad assortment of local flavors are woven into its sweet threads. My version is tropical, a swirly periwinkle tower made of ube, as soft as velvet. Crème Chantilly (the fancy French name for whipped cream) is tucked inside. And a mound of glossy macapuno sits on top like a radiant alabaster cherry. You don't need to be a Michelin-starred chef to make this. Though once you're finished, you might feel like one.

For the pastry: In a large bowl, whisk together the flour, powdered sugar, and salt. Add the butter and toss to coat. Using your hands, rub the butter into the flour mixture until crumbly. Add the egg yolks and stir with a fork, mashing the yolks into the mixture, until well combined. Do the same thing with the water. Knead by hand, in the bowl, until the dough comes together.

Shape the dough into a flat disc and wrap in plastic wrap. Refrigerate for at least 1 hour.

Meanwhile, arrange six 4-inch (10 cm) tart tins with removable bottoms on a sheet pan and grease with cooking spray. Cut six 6-inch (15 cm) squares of foil.

Divide the dough into 6 equal portions (about 75 g each). Shape each portion into a flat disc. Lightly flour a work surface and roll out each portion into a 6-inch (15 cm) round.

Press the rounds into the prepared tins, making sure the dough is snug against the crevices. (After you've lined the first tin, make a little ball out of the scraps and use it to press the pastry into the remaining tins). Trim away the excess dough with a sharp knife.

Prick the dough all over with a fork. Line each pastry tart with a square of foil, pressing into the crevices, so it covers the dough entirely. Fill with dried beans or pie weights. Refrigerate for at least 30 minutes.

MAKES SIX 4-INCH (10 CM) TARTS

Pastry Crust

2 cups (250 g) all-purpose flour, plus extra for dusting

¼ cup (25 g) powdered sugar

½ teaspoon kosher salt

1 stick (113 g) unsalted butter

2 large egg yolks

3 tablespoons (45 g) water

Coconut Filling

1 cup plus 2 tablespoons (90 g) store-bought whipped cream

1 cup plus 1 tablespoon (53 g) unsweetened finely shredded coconut (see Note)

Ube Filling and Garnish

¾ cup (186 g) ube halaya, at room temperature

¼ teaspoon ube paste

⅛ teaspoon kosher salt

6 tablespoons (30 g) store-bought whipped cream

Unsweetened finely shredded coconut, for garnish (see Note)

Jarred macapuno, for garnish

Special Equipment

Six 4-inch (10 cm) tart tins with removable bottoms

Note: To finely shred the coconut, pulse a few times in a small food processor. It's not necessary, but you've come this far.

I love how it feigns fancy because in reality you can be a little messy about it and still end up with a very dramatic presentation.

Meanwhile, preheat the oven to 350°F (180°C).

Bake until the dough starts to look dry with a matte finish, 20 to 25 minutes. Remove the foil and beans and bake until golden all over, 15 to 20 minutes.

Note: After you remove the foil and beans and return the pastry to the oven, it should not balloon in the center. If it does, put the foil and beans back and bake for another 5 minutes before continuing.

Transfer the sheet pan to a wire rack and let cool for 15 minutes. Remove the pastry shells from the tins and transfer them to the wire rack to cool completely.

For the coconut filling: In a medium bowl, stir together the whipped cream and shredded coconut.

For the ube filling: In a medium bowl, using a hand mixer, beat together the ube halaya, ube paste, and salt until well combined. Fold in the whipped cream. Transfer to a large piping bag fitted with a small round tip (Wilton #5).

To assemble: Divide the coconut filling among the cooled pastry shells (about 3 tablespoons [5 g] each) and shape into a dome using a small offset spatula.

Starting at the bottom of each tart and working up, pipe a single layer of the ube filling over the whipped cream dome. (Don't worry if there are gaps. This doesn't have to be perfect). Pipe on a second layer of the ube filling onto each tart, covering up any gaps. (Again, don't worry about perfection. Messy chic is the vibe).

Garnish with a shower of shredded coconut and top with macapuno. Serve immediately or refrigerate overnight. ●

Star Fruit Tarts

I'm just as intrigued by star fruit today as I was when I was a child. There are almost a dozen trees on my mom's family farm. Gleaming yellow shapes juxtaposed against verdant green leaves, practically calling out with their colors as if they're saying, "pick me." Slicing one reveals a five-pointed star, which tastes bright and sweet with a whisper of citrus. They're delicious raw, but you can cook them, too. I like to boil them down, skin and all, into a glossy jam. This does dull its organic acidity, but a measure of lemon juice restores that sour tingle. With the jam packed into golden shortbread crusts and topped with a sweet, shining star, these tiny tarts look like the tropical version of British mince pies. Call it a compromise for both sets of my grandparents.

For the pastry: In a large bowl, whisk together the flour, sugar, and salt. Add the butter and toss to coat. Using your hands, rub the butter into the flour mixture until crumbly. Add the egg yolks and stir with a fork, mashing the yolks into the mixture, until well combined. Do the same thing with the water. Knead by hand, in the bowl, until the dough comes together.

Shape the dough into a flat disc and wrap in plastic wrap. Refrigerate for at least 30 minutes.

For the filling: Trim away a small sliver from the ends of a star fruit. Halve lengthwise, then cut lengthwise into 5 spears. Remove the seeds with a fork. Cut each spear into two thin spears. Repeat with 2 more star fruits. Gather the spears and cut into a medium dice. You should have about 14 ounces (400 g) total.

Trim away a small sliver from the ends of the remaining star fruit. Cut crosswise into scant ¼-inch (½ cm) slices and remove the seeds with a fork. Set aside.

In a small saucepan, add the diced star fruit and sugar. Stir with a fork until it starts looking juicy. Let macerate for 30 minutes. Stir in the salt.

Bring to a steady simmer over medium heat. Cook, stirring occasionally, until the juice has reduced slightly and the fruit is tender and starting to break down, about 10 minutes. Adjust the heat as needed to maintain a simmer (not a boil or a rapid simmer).

Meanwhile, in a small bowl, whisk together the cornstarch and water.

Stir the cornstarch mixture into the saucepan. Cook over medium-low heat, stirring constantly, until thick and glazy (like a peach pie filling), about 2 minutes.

Remove from the heat and stir in the lemon zest and lemon juice. Transfer to a medium bowl and let cool to room temperature. Refrigerate until chilled, about 1 hour.

To assemble the tarts: Grease a 12-cup muffin tin with cooking spray.

Lightly flour a work surface and roll out the dough into a 14-inch (36 cm) round. Using a 3 ½-inch (9 cm) round cutter, stamp out 12 rounds, gathering the scraps and rerolling as needed.

MAKES 12 SMALL TARTS

Pastry Crust

2 cups (250 g) all-purpose flour, plus extra for dusting

¼ cup (25 g) powdered sugar

½ teaspoon kosher salt

1 stick (113 g) unsalted butter

2 large egg yolks

¼ cup (60 g) water

Filling and Garnish

4 ripe yellow star fruit (about 20 oz. [567 g]), divided

¼ cup plus 2 tablespoons (75 g) granulated sugar

⅛ teaspoon kosher salt

1 tablespoon (8 g) cornstarch

3 tablespoons (45 g) water

Grated zest of 1 lemon

1½ tablespoons (22 g) fresh lemon juice

A tropical version of British mince pies

Press a dough round into each of the prepared muffin cups, making sure the dough is snug against the crevices. (A little ball of scrap dough helps with this). The dough will only extend about halfway up the sides.

Divide the star fruit filling evenly among the pastry shells (about 1½ tablespoons [30 g] each). Top with a star fruit slice and refrigerate for 30 minutes.

Meanwhile, preheat the oven to 400°F (200°C).

Bake until the crust is golden and the star fruit slice is starting to darken at the tips, about 30 minutes.

Transfer the tin to a wire rack and let cool for 15 minutes. Remove the tarts from the tin and transfer them to the wire rack. Enjoy slightly warm or at room temperature. ●

Biko Coconut Custard Pie

Biko has always been my favorite Filipino kakanin (rice cake). It's made from sticky rice grains bound by latik (the coconut caramel version) and topped with either more caramel or crunchy coconut curds (the other version of latik). Every time I see my family, whether it's the holidays or an ordinary visit there's always Biko.

Here, the rice cake functions as a "crust" that's still very much gooey and gummy. A stream of coconut custard is poured into the hollow. And as it bakes, the biko merges into a sticky barrier while the custard sets up soft and creamy in the center. Every bite delivers that classic chew with a lush and velvety finish.

MAKES ONE 9-INCH (23 CM) PIE

Soaked Coconut

½ cup (120 g) canned unsweetened coconut milk

½ cup (25 g) unsweetened shredded coconut

Biko Crust

1 cup (200 g) sticky rice

1 cup (240 g) water , plus extra for rinsing the rice

⅓ cup (90 g) canned unsweetened coconut milk

¼ cup (50 g) dark brown sugar

Pinch of kosher salt

Custard Filling

1 large egg

½ cup (100 g) granulated sugar

1 tablespoon (8 g) all-purpose flour

2 teaspoons vanilla bean paste or extract

Pinch of kosher salt

For the soaked coconut: In a small saucepan, stir together the coconut milk and shredded coconut. Bring to a boil over high heat. Remove from the heat, cover, and set aside to soak while you make the biko crust.

For the biko crust: In a medium bowl, add the rice and enough water to cover and swish your hand around in the bowl until the water turns a milky, cloudy white. Drain through a fine-mesh sieve and repeat two more times.

Transfer the rice to a medium saucepan and add the 1 cup (240 g) of water (the water might be a little opaque but you should be able to see the rice clearly). Cover with a lid and bring to a boil over high heat. Reduce to a simmer and cook until the rice is tender and the water is absorbed, 12 to 15 minutes. Remove from the heat and set aside (with the lid on).

In a medium nonstick skillet, whisk together the coconut milk, brown sugar, and salt. Bring to a boil over high heat, watching to make sure it doesn't bubble over. Reduce to a simmer over medium heat and cook, stirring occasionally, until dark and thick and reduced to somewhere between ⅓ and ½ cup (80 and 120 ml), 2 to 3 minutes.

Turn off the heat and add the latik back into the pan. Stir in the cooked sticky rice until well combined. Turn the heat on to medium and cook, stirring constantly, until the latik is absorbed and the mixture is thick and sticky, about 2 minutes.

Grease a 9-inch (23 cm) pie plate with cooking spray. Transfer the biko to the plate and press into the bottom and sides with a silicone spatula. (This doesn't have to be perfect quite yet). Set aside to cool for 10 minutes.

Meanwhile, preheat the oven to 375°F (190°C).

Set the pie plate on a sheet pan. Lightly coat your hands with cooking spray and shape up the biko crust, making sure it's nice and even.

For the custard filling: In the saucepan with the soaked coconut mixture, whisk in the egg. Next whisk in the sugar, flour, vanilla, and salt. Pour the mixture into the biko crust.

Bake until the custard is just set, does not jiggle, and a toothpick inserted into the center of the custard comes out mostly clean, 25 to 30 minutes.

Transfer the pie plate to a wire rack and let cool for at least 20 minutes before slicing. Enjoy slightly warm, at room temperature, or chilled.

Cover with plastic wrap and store in the refrigerator or wrap individual portions in plastic wrap and freeze. Frozen portions can be thawed in the refrigerator overnight and warmed in the microwave. ●

The Price of Paradise

The Legend and Real Story of the Philippines

Philippine legend claims that the world, when it first began, had no land. There was only the sea and the sky, which stretched across existence in parallel pools of infinite blue. Between them, an onyx bird sailed on her wings up and around, back and forth, until she grew tired and weary. The bird flew farther and farther, sweeping across great lengths of distance, in search of a place to rest. But there was nothing. So, she decided to start a quarrel. The bird soared up to the sky and down to the sea, telling each the other wished them harm. The sea and the sky became angry, just as the bird had hoped. And she urged the two on, fueling their fury.

It was the sea that broke first. Its sapphire waters darkened to a stormy shade of silver that churned with agitated rage. The sea started to rise, gradually building its stature until it was as steep and sturdy as a cliff wall. The colossal wave curled menacingly, surging with liquid vibration, and threw down its weight, crashing with violence.

In response, the bright, cobalt sky blurred into a murky, thunderous haze. Charged with anger, it hurled a cascade of enormous rocks onto the water. The sea attempted to stand, but the heavy stones fell like rain. They plunged into its depths and piled into mountainous heaps, creating many islands. The sea and the sky finally agreed to end their war. Green trickled across the fresh ground, materializing into colorful blossoms, twisted vines, and wild jungles. The bird was pleased with her efforts, and she steered toward the land as the dismal gray canvas faded into a brilliant, cheerful blue.

The bird rested in the trees, coasted on the breeze, and warmed her feathers in the sun. As she glided along the shore, the bird discovered a large stalk of bamboo. She alighted on it, then walked around it, inspecting its structure. The bird plunged her beak into the woody stem until it burst open. And out came a man and a woman, the very first people.

I love this story because, to me, it captures the soul of the Philippines and its people. It reveals the synergy between great beauty and great adversity, and how humanity was born out of conflict into an unimaginable world.

The real story of the Philippines isn't so different. Its borders have withstood weather and war, ruin and reign. To its earliest conquerors—resting under the islands' towering palms, bathing in its gentle blue lagoons, and eating its sweet, fleshy mangoes and juicy orbs of pink guava—it must have felt like they'd been transported to a place of very real fairy tales. A paradise beyond compare.

Here, mountains, cliffs, and caves carve the land, glittering with emerald jungles and cerulean beaches. A parade of hibiscus, jade vine, orchids, and jasmine infuse the air, mixing its sweet scent with the tropical fruit and nuts that hang in abundance all around. Electric-colored birds float among the treetops, four-legged creatures wander the terrain, and beneath the surface of the glassy waters are schools of radiant fish and rainbow coral reefs whittled into sculptures. In this corner of existence, the land is fruitful and the views are mesmerizing.

Of course, no fairy tale is complete without an antagonist, its source of conflict. And in this story, the hero and villain are one and the same. For the thing that makes the Philippines such a paradise, threatens its very existence. The ocean contorts its body into wicked typhoons, spinning the wind and sea into furious cyclones. Tsunamis raise the waters into giant waves that break with vigor, drowning everything in their path. Below the island floor, the Earth simmers like a cauldron, oozing with liquid fire. Volcanoes stew into violent eruptions, spitting lava and the promise of death. With great beauty comes great cost. Because nature, as they say, always keeps its balance.

The Philippines lives within these two extremes: magnificent beauty and life-threatening peril. That conflict, ever present, has shaped the very essence of the land, its people, and its culture. Filipinos are known for their sparkling personalities, enthusiasm for fun, generous hospitality, and never taking life too seriously. Even in

The author's mother (far right) with her family on the farm after a typhoon.

the face of complete loss, they band fiercely together to reshape and evolve and overcome. They're acutely resilient and fighting for what they believe in is in their blood. And since the beginning of time, they've lived with the land, relying on its bountiful resources while at the same time threatened by them.

During the last Ice Age, continental glaciers covered the Earth in panels of white, building cliffs of crystal and swallowing the sea. Ground emerged where it hadn't before. And it's believed that the first inhabitants of the Philippines walked over these land bridges from neighboring territories such as present-day Australia, Malaysia, and Indonesia. Whether these wanderers planned to stay is not known. But rising waters washed away their road home and so, stranded as they were, they established a new life. These indigenous groups thrived as hunter-gatherers, mastered the art of jungle survival, and coexisted with nature. They believed that all things—be it a forest, the weather, or a single rock—possessed a spiritual essence. In time, Chinese and Arab merchants dropped anchor along the islands' coastlines, trading fine porcelain and silks in exchange for beeswax and deer horn. The Chinese eventually settled in great numbers, as did the Arab Muslims, who converted many southern communities to Islam.

In these early days, the Philippines was not a united nation but rather a region populated by numerous self-governing tribes. Alliances turned neighbors into enemies, betrayal led to war, and all were in constant competition for the islands' rich bounty. Over time, many different languages, customs, and beliefs developed among its people.

By the sixteenth century, Ferdinand Magellan, a Portuguese captain sailing for Spain, set his eyes on fame, fortune, and outshining the glory of Christopher Columbus. He planned to map a western sea passage to the Spice Islands, an expedition never done before. On a brisk late-summer day in 1519, a fleet of five stately ships set sail across the open waters around the world. There were nearly 270 men aboard, each sharply aware of the arduous journey ahead. Life at sea was marked by storms, starvation, scurvy, and strife. Magellan was gritty, adventurous, and as ruthless as a pirate. He was feared and reviled by most of his crew. Those who dared to defy the grim captain were beheaded, quartered, shackled in chains, or abandoned on islands.

Two years later, just before reaching the Spice Islands, Magellan chanced upon the Philippine shores. The crew was instantly bewitched by their newly found paradise. The sun melted into the sand in warm, golden rays. Colorful fruits beckoned to be plucked. And the breeze brushed blissfully through the palms. Within days Magellan had befriended a native tribe and, after converting them to Christianity, agreed to aid their chieftain, Datu Zula, in defeating a rival clan.

The captain's crew pleaded against it, but Magellan was certain the primitive defenses were no match for their weapons. Some forty-nine men advanced toward the island of Mactan, wading through thick waters before reaching land. They'd grossly underestimated their enemy. More than 1,500 tribal warriors, howling with loud, excited yelps, charged toward the Spaniards. Magellan's army uselessly fired off their muskets while the natives hurled everything from bamboo spears, heavy stones, and iron blades. Once Magellan was identified as the leader, he became the primary target and every effort was made to assassinate him. Amid the chaos and clamor of battle, a poison arrow cut through the air into the captain's body. With their commander dead, the Spaniards retreated, leaving Magellan's corpse behind.

Only one ship and eighteen men returned safely to Spain and the Empire vowed revenge. After several attempts, Spain eventually conquered the tribal land and ruled for over three hundred years. Spain consolidated the islands under a single governing body and founded the new nation in the name of their sovereign, King Philip II.

Determined to spread their way of life, the Spaniards destroyed many Philippine artifacts and historical writings. Spanish infiltrated the language, new customs were introduced, and ornate cathedrals cropped up across the land. One of the greatest impacts of Spain's authority was the installation of Catholicism, which continues to thrive today, making the Philippines the only Asian country to recognize Christianity as its primary religion.

It's likely that one of the best ways to understand a culture is through its food. Chinese immigrants brought various cooking techniques to Filipino kitchens and contributed dishes like pancit (stir-fried noodles), buchi (sesame balls), and lumpia (spring rolls). American soldiers introduced the islands to canned meats, like Spam and corned beef, which were quickly adopted as permanent fixtures. But the greatest culinary influence hails from Spain, to which nearly 80 percent of Filipino cuisine can be traced back.

In 1898, after the Spanish-American War, Spain ceded the Philippines to the United States. The Pacific nation desperately desired to govern themselves and eventually plans were fashioned to make it so. But World War II brought Japan to the islands and they almost instantly seized control. Violence continued for years and the Philippines was left damaged in its aftermath. The nation gathered its strength, acquired from centuries of fortitude, and on July 4, 1946, the Philippines was, at last, granted full independence. Despite this feat, the Philippines recognizes June 12—the day the islands gained freedom from Spanish rule—as their national Independence Day.

There does seem to be a peculiar, underlying equilibrium within our world. A sort of checks and balances that nature and humanity commands. The ocean tide goes in and out. The sun rises and sets. Can there truly be peace without war? Courage without fear? Love without loss? There's a rare type of beauty that stems from tension. Almost as if there's a price to pay for the extraordinary. A particle that invades an oyster causes so much agitation a pearl is formed. A rainbow follows a storm. A lotus blooms in the mud. The story of the Philippines is riddled with tension. Yet it's managed to maintain unbelievable landscapes, preserve lavish coastlines, generate its own unique culture, and produce some of the most exceptional people. ●

04

Puddings, Custards & Jellies

Mango Float Cheesecake Cups

My mom likes to text my sister and me every year to let us know when yellow mangoes are in season, a habit she started when I left for college. We've come to expect it as much as the annual Happy Birthday message. As soon as she spots one at her grocery store, she'll text our group chat, using the mango emoji (which is green so she types YELLOW in all caps). They've always been a favorite in my family. Sweet and juicy and supple like jelly, they're the star of this icebox cake, also called mango royale or crema de mangga. My take on this dessert swirls cream cheese into the base, adding body and tang, reshuffling its layers into a spoonable cheesecake. I stack the tiers into individual glasses, simulating dainty parfaits or trifles, which makes for very pretty presentation and tidy portions. As it rests in the refrigerator, the filling thickens and the graham cracker crumbs grow tender, drinking in the creamy mixture. Do use the ripest mangoes you can find. They have the best flavor.

MAKES 4 SERVINGS

¼ cup (60 g) heavy cream

4 oz. (113 g) cream cheese, at room temperature

¼ cup (80 g) sweetened condensed milk

Grated zest of 1 lemon

1½ teaspoons (7 g) fresh lemon juice

1 teaspoon vanilla extract

Pinch of kosher salt

½ cup (50 g) finely ground graham cracker crumbs

⅔ cup (125 g) diced Ataulfo yellow mango

In the bowl of a stand mixer fitted with the whisk, beat the heavy cream on medium-high speed until stiff peaks form, 1 to 2 minutes. Transfer to a small bowl and set aside.

In the same stand mixer bowl (no need to clean), add the cream cheese, sweetened condensed milk, lemon zest, lemon juice, vanilla, and salt. Beat on medium-high speed until smooth and creamy, 1 to 2 minutes. Fold in the whipped cream in two additions.

Add 3 tablespoons (30 g) of the cream cheese mixture to the bottom of each of the four 5-ounce dessert glasses.

Top each with 1 tablespoon (6 g) of graham cracker crumbs followed by 1 tablespoon (15 g) of diced mango.

Repeat the layers once more with the remaining cream cheese, graham cracker crumbs, and mango.

Place the glasses on a sheet pan and cover with plastic wrap. Refrigerate until the filling is set and the graham cracker crumbs are softened, at least 3 hours, but overnight is best. ●

Mango trees at the author's family farm in the Philippines

Blueberry Jasmine Taho Pudding

Because I grew up in a coastal town, the water was a large part of my childhood entertainment. When we were kids, my sister and I would fill plastic pails with sand and ocean water and lug them around singing, "Taho! Taho! It's off to work we go!" mimicking the familiar tune from Walt Disney's *Snow White and the Seven Dwarves*. The muse for our melodic genius was, of course, the many taho street vendors throughout the Philippines. These peddlers can be spotted drifting through neighborhoods with a long pole set over their shoulders, a large metal bucket dangling from each end, calling out, "Tahooooo!" with assured emphasis. The warm silken tofu snack is traditionally prepared with sago (but I opt for tapioca since it's easier to find) and flavored with a brown sugar simple syrup called arnibal. But some hawkers sell specialty flavors like strawberry, ube, and mango graham.

My version leans on fresh blueberry sauce, steeped with jasmine tea for a delicate floral finish, and large black sugar boba pearls for a soft, bouncy bite. The tofu is whipped into a creamy pudding and steals heat, upon assembly, from the warm fruity sauce. Gently swirled, their colors bleed into each other, forging shades of purple that shift from plum to iris to lavender.

In a food processor, add the silken tofu, 2 tablespoons (25 g) of the sugar, and the vanilla. Puree until smooth. Set aside.

In a liquid measuring cup, add the boiling water and jasmine tea bag and let steep for 2 minutes.

Discard the tea bag and pour the jasmine tea into a large saucepan. Add the blueberries, remaining ½ cup (100 g) of sugar, and the salt. Bring to a boil over medium-high heat and cook until the blueberries begin to soften, about 3 minutes.

Meanwhile, in a small bowl, whisk together the cornstarch and cold water.

Stir the cornstarch mixture into the saucepan. Reduce to a simmer and cook, stirring occasionally, until saucy and slightly thickened, 3 to 4 minutes. Remove from the heat and let cool for 10 minutes.

Meanwhile, prepare the boba according to the package directions. Cool the boba by rinsing with cold water and drain well.

Dividing evenly, add the boba to four 10-ounce (300 ml) jars. Then top with the silken tofu followed by the blueberry sauce. Serve immediately. ●

MAKES 4 SERVINGS

One 16 oz. (454 g) package silken tofu

½ cup (100 g) plus 2 tablespoons (25 g) granulated sugar, divided

1 teaspoon vanilla bean paste or extract

1 cup (240 g) boiling water

1 jasmine tea bag

16 oz. (454 g) fresh or frozen blueberries (about 3 cups)

⅛ teaspoon kosher salt

2 teaspoons (6 g) cornstarch

1 tablespoon (15 g) cold water

1 cup (160 g) black sugar boba pearls

Note: You can make all the components, except the boba, ahead of time. Prepare the boba right before you're ready to assemble and reheat the blueberry sauce.

Pumpkin Orange Blossom Leche Flan

This recipe marries American pumpkin pie with Filipino leche flan, a rich and custardy creme caramel. Scented with orange blossom and fresh citrus zest, it's brisk and fragrant like a cool autumn night. The pumpkin puree, spiced with cinnamon and ginger, lends a mellow, vegetal flavor and creates a thicker consistency than classic leche flan. I melt the sugar for the caramel directly in an aluminum cake pan, swirling it over the heat of a gas stove burner just like my mom does (please, use oven mitts). I find it easier to manipulate into an even layer and creates one less dish to wash. The caramel, which expands as it hardens, cracks under the pressure of being in a vessel too small (you'll hear it, if you're listening), leaving thin fissures on the surface like fragile ice. Once the leche flan is baked and chilled, it's inverted onto a platter. Liquid gold streams brilliantly down the sides and the surface gleams with an amber pool of caramel so clear you can almost see your reflection in it.

MAKES ONE 9-INCH (23 CM) FLAN

1 orange

One 12 fl. oz. (355 ml) can evaporated milk

¾ cup (150 g) granulated sugar

Whole milk, as needed

10 large egg yolks

One 14 oz. (396 g) can sweetened condensed milk

½ cup (115 g) canned pumpkin puree

2 teaspoons orange blossom water

½ teaspoon ground ginger

½ teaspoon ground cinnamon

¼ teaspoon kosher salt

Using a Y-peeler, peel off strips of orange zest from the orange and remove any excess pith with a paring knife. (Set the peeled orange aside for later). In a small saucepan, add the orange zest and evaporated milk and bring to a boil over high heat. As soon as it boils, remove from the heat and cover. Let steep for 15 minutes.

To a 9-inch (23 cm) round aluminum cake pan, add the sugar and shake the pan so it spreads into an even layer.

Wearing oven mitts, hold the pan over medium heat on a gas stovetop and cook, tilting the pan, until the sugar is melted and golden, about 5 minutes. (You can set the pan aside periodically and move the sugar around with a silicone spatula to help it along). If you don't have a gas stovetop, you can heat the sugar in a small saucepan over medium heat until it melts and pour it into the cake pan.

Place the cake pan in a large roasting pan and let the sugar harden (it may crack as it sets).

Strain the orange-infused milk through a fine-mesh sieve into a 2-cup (500 ml) liquid measuring cup. Add enough orange juice (using the peeled orange) to make 1½ cups (350 ml) liquid total (you can supplement with whole milk, if needed). Transfer the mixture to a large bowl and let cool to room temperature, about 15 minutes.

Meanwhile, preheat the oven to 350°F (180°C). Bring a large kettle of water to a boil (enough for the roasting pan).

To the large bowl with the infused evaporated milk, add the egg yolks, sweetened condensed milk, pumpkin puree, orange blossom water, ginger, cinnamon, and salt. Whisk to combine.

Strain the mixture through a fine-mesh sieve into the cake pan with the hardened caramel. Add enough boiling water to the roasting pan to come halfway up the sides of the cake pan.

(Recipe continued on following page).

(Pumpkin Orange Blossom Leche Flan continued from previous page).

Carefully transfer to the oven and bake until the leche flan is set and a tooth-pick inserted into the center of the flan comes out clean, about 50 minutes.

Transfer the cake pan to a wire rack and let cool to room temperature. Cover with foil and refrigerate until completely chilled, at least 6 hours, but overnight is best.

Run a small offset spatula around the perimeter to loosen the edges. Invert the leche flan onto a cake plate or serving platter. ●

The surface gleams with an amber pool of caramel so clear you can almost see your reflection in it.

Chocolate and Milk Jelly Panna Cotta

I had panna cotta for the first time at twenty-three. A recent college grad, I was visiting Venice. My friend and I had just stepped off the ferry when a sudden storm pushed us inside a cramped brick restaurant. The room, lit by candlelight, flickered in shadow and bronze. The food was delicious. I noticed a server carrying a tray of desserts—small white mounds dribbled with chocolate—to a corner table, where a father and son sat silently, rolling loose tobacco in paper. I ordered one right away. It was cool and creamy, delicate like soft milky gel.

This texture, forever ingrained in my taste memory, is applied to Filipino chocolate and milk jelly, a two-tiered wheel of thick gelatin. My version is softer, silkier. A spoon can carve through it without any resistance. Condensed milk sweetens the layer of vanilla, and cocoa powder saturates the layer of chocolate. There are few flavor combinations as straightforward as chocolate and vanilla. That's what makes it so perfect. Pairing something light and creamy against something dark and rich.

For the vanilla layer: To a small saucepan, add the milk, sweetened condensed milk, sugar, and salt. Cook over medium heat, whisking occasionally, until the sugar is dissolved and the mixture is steaming, about 5 minutes. Remove from the heat and whisk in the vanilla. Cover to keep warm.

To a small bowl, add the water and sprinkle the gelatin evenly over the top. Whisk together and let absorb for 5 minutes.

Add the gelatin to the warm milk mixture and whisk until dissolved. Strain through a fine-mesh sieve into a 2-cup (500 ml) liquid measuring cup.

Divide the mixture evenly among four 4-ounce (120 ml) glass bowls or ramekins. Place the ramekins on a sheet pan and refrigerate until just barely set, about 30 minutes.

For the chocolate layer: In a small saucepan, add the cream, sugar, cocoa powder, coffee powder, and salt. Cook over medium heat, whisking occasionally, until the sugar is dissolved and the mixture is steaming, about 5 minutes. Cover to keep warm.

Pour the water into a small bowl and sprinkle the gelatin evenly over the top. Whisk together and let absorb for 5 minutes.

Add the gelatin to the warm cream mixture and whisk until dissolved. Strain through a fine-mesh sieve into a 2-cup (500 ml) liquid measuring cup.

Dividing evenly, pour the chocolate mixture on top of the set vanilla mixture. Cover with plastic wrap and refrigerate until fully set, at least 3 hours and up to overnight.

Fill a medium bowl with boiling water. Working with one at a time, dip the bowls or ramekins in the boiling water for about 15 seconds. Carefully run a small offset spatula around the perimeter (go only halfway deep or you'll spread the chocolate layer into the vanilla). Invert onto a dessert plate. (If the chocolate does run into the vanilla, you can clean it up by scraping gently with the offset spatula). ●

MAKES 4 SERVINGS

Vanilla Layer

½ cup (120 g) whole milk

½ cup (160 g) sweetened condensed milk

1 tablespoon (12 g) granulated sugar

Pinch of kosher salt

½ teaspoon vanilla bean paste or extract

1 tablespoon (15 g) cold water

¾ teaspoon unflavored gelatin powder

Chocolate Layer

1 cup (240 g) heavy cream

⅓ cup (66 g) granulated sugar

1 ½ tablespoons (18 g) unsweetened Dutch process cocoa powder

¼ teaspoon instant coffee or espresso powder

Pinch of kosher salt

1 tablespoon (15 g) cold water

¾ teaspoon unflavored gelatin powder

Note: You can make the panna cottas 2 days in advance and unmold them 3 hours before serving (as long as they're stored in the refrigerator).

Mango Sago Brûlée

Some call it a drink. Others say it's a soup. My take on mango sago, a milky tapioca dessert, is decidedly a crème brûlée, made with fresh chunks of ripe yellow mango, coconut custard, and a golden mirror of torched brown sugar. The custard might seem loose at first (compared to a pudding), but the bouncy beads of tapioca reinforce its structure. The terms sago and tapioca are often used interchangeably, and they function the same way. But if we're being technical about it, they aren't *exactly* the same thing. Tapioca pearls are made from yuca (cassava) root and sago pearls are made from the starch of certain palm trees. It's easier for me to find tapioca, but you're welcome to use either. What I love most about this dish is the contrast in temperature and texture. How the crunchy and brittle top gives way to the cool silky filling and bright fleshy mango beneath.

MAKES 6 SERVINGS

14 oz. (400 g) diced yellow Ataulfo mango (about 2 cups)

5 cups (1200 g) water

¼ cup (48 g) small pearl tapioca

1 cup (240 g) canned unsweetened coconut milk, divided

1 tablespoon (8 g) cornstarch

2 large egg yolks, at room temperature

¼ cup (50 g) granulated sugar

¼ teaspoon kosher salt

1 tablespoon (14 g) unsalted butter, at room temperature

1 tablespoon (15 g) fresh lemon juice

12 teaspoons (60 g) turbinado sugar

Special Equipment

Six 4 oz. (120 ml) ramekins

Kitchen torch (see Note)

Note: If you don't have a kitchen torch, you can use your oven broiler to caramelize the sugar.

Place six 4-ounce (120 ml) ramekins on a sheet pan. Divide the diced mango evenly among the ramekins.

In a large saucepan, bring the water to a boil over high heat. Stir in the tapioca and bring back to a boil. Cook, stirring occasionally, until tender and translucent, about 20 minutes. Strain the tapioca through a fine-mesh sieve and rinse with cold water. Set aside.

In a medium bowl, whisk together ¼ cup (60 g) of the coconut milk and the cornstarch. Whisk in the egg yolks and set beside the stovetop.

In a small saucepan, whisk together the remaining ¾ cup (180 g) of coconut milk, the granulated sugar, and salt. Heat over medium heat until warm and steaming, 3 to 4 minutes. Turn off the heat.

Gradually whisk the warm coconut milk mixture into the yolk mixture. Pour it back into the saucepan and cook over medium heat, whisking constantly, until it's thick enough to coat the back of a spoon and has the consistency of a smooth pourable custard (not like a pudding), about 3 minutes. (You'll think it looks too thin, but the tapioca will add just enough body).

Remove from the heat and whisk in the tapioca, butter, and lemon juice.

Divide the mixture evenly among the ramekins and cover with plastic wrap. Refrigerate until chilled and set, at least 6 hours, but overnight is best.

Before serving, let the ramekins sit out at room temperature for 10 minutes. Sprinkle each ramekin with 2 teaspoons (10 g) of turbinado sugar. Caramelize the sugar with a kitchen torch. ●

Sticky Latik Pudding

In Philippine cuisine, latik has two identities. Depending on the region, it can refer to crispy coconut curds or a syrupy coconut caramel sauce. And although I could eat the latter with a shovel, adding a smidge of cake makes this seem a little more respectable. The solution: an island version of sticky toffee pudding. The cake is lavishly spiced, plush, and baked into snug little muffins made extra moist with creamy, mashed bananas—you want to use the ripest ones, brown and spotted. Beyond the latik sauce, which tastes like nutty brown sugar, these tiny cakes are also served with a slick coconut custard (because I love custard and more is more). It should both be smooth and able to cascade off a spoon in a thick, continuous stream. There's plenty of each. Because I'm a firm believer that you can never have enough sauce.

For the coconut custard: In a medium bowl, whisk together ¼ cup (60 g) of the coconut milk and the cornstarch. Whisk in the egg yolks and set beside the stovetop.

In a small saucepan, whisk together the remaining coconut milk, the sugar, and salt. Heat over medium heat until warm and steaming, about 5 minutes. Turn off the heat.

Gradually whisk the warm coconut milk mixture into the yolk mixture. Pour it back into the saucepan and cook over medium-high heat, whisking constantly, until it's thick enough to coat the back of a spoon and has the consistency of a smooth pourable custard (not like a pudding), 3 to 5 minutes.

Remove from the heat and whisk in the vanilla. Transfer the custard to a medium bowl or large liquid measuring cup. You should have about 1 ¾ cups (445 g). Cover with plastic wrap so it touches the surface of the custard directly (this will prevent a skin from forming). Set aside at room temperature.

For the latik sauce: In a medium nonstick skillet, whisk together the coconut milk, brown sugar, and salt. Bring to a boil over high heat, watching to make sure it doesn't bubble over.

Reduce to a simmer over medium-low heat and cook, stirring occasionally, until dark and thick and reduced to about 1 ⅔ cups (480 g), about 15 minutes. Transfer the latik sauce to a medium bowl or large liquid measuring cup. Cover with foil and keep warm.

For the banana cake: Preheat the oven to 350°F (180°C). Lightly grease 9 cups of a 12-cup muffin tin with cooking spray.

In a medium bowl, whisk together the flour, cinnamon, baking powder, baking soda, ginger, nutmeg, salt, and cloves.

In a large bowl, using a hand mixer, beat the brown sugar, oil, molasses, and vanilla on medium-high speed until thick and fluffy, 3 to 4 minutes. Beat in the egg. Beat in the mashed bananas. Add the flour mixture in two additions, beating each addition on low speed until just combined.

MAKES 9 SERVINGS

Coconut Custard

One 13.5 fl. oz. (400 ml) can unsweetened coconut milk, divided

1 tablespoon (8 g) cornstarch

2 large egg yolks, at room temperature

⅓ cup (66 g) granulated sugar

¼ teaspoon kosher salt

½ teaspoon vanilla extract

Latik Sauce

One 13.5 fl. oz. (400 ml) can unsweetened coconut milk

1 cup (200 g) dark brown sugar

¼ teaspoon kosher salt

Banana Cake

¾ cup plus 2 tablespoons (110 g) all-purpose flour

1 teaspoon ground cinnamon

¾ teaspoon baking powder

½ teaspoon baking soda

½ teaspoon ground ginger

¼ teaspoon freshly grated nutmeg

¼ teaspoon kosher salt

Pinch of ground cloves

½ cup (100 g) dark brown sugar

3 tablespoons (39 g) neutral oil

2 tablespoons (44 g) molasses

½ teaspoon vanilla extract

1 large egg, at room temperature

2 very ripe bananas, mashed (about 1 cup [226 g]) total

Divide the batter evenly among the prepared muffin cups (about 60 g each).

Bake until puffed and a toothpick inserted into the center of the cakes comes out mostly clean with a few sticky crumbs, 18 to 20 minutes. Transfer the muffin tin to a wire rack and let cool for 5 minutes. Run a small offset spatula around the perimeter of each cake to loosen the edges. Invert onto the wire rack.

Before serving, reheat the coconut custard and latik sauce if needed. All the components (including the cake) should be warm.

To assemble each serving: Pour about 3 tablespoons (55 g) of the coconut custard into a shallow dessert bowl. Place a cake (upside down) in the center of the custard. Spoon about 2 ½ tablespoons (45 g) of the latik sauce over top.

If you're preparing ahead of time or have leftovers, store the cakes at room temperature in an airtight container. Refrigerate the coconut custard and the latik sauce. Reheat all the components before serving. ●

Black Forest Champorado

Some of the best desserts are the ones that double as breakfast foods. Champorado, a chocolate rice pudding, is one of them. It's genuinely a porridge, made with rice rather than oats. And not just any rice. Sticky glutinous rice. This makes the finished texture thick and viscous, almost stretchy. A pinch of espresso enhances the chocolate while a dash of vanilla softens its natural bitterness. My interpretation is dressed first with whipped cream, which gives in to the heat, melting into a milky puddle. A dollop of sour cherry sauce, shining like red patent leather, settles on top. And a sprinkle of toasted coconut flakes adds a brittle, nutty finish. I like to keep extra nearby to scatter onto each spoonful.

MAKES ABOUT 1 QUART (1 LITER)

Champorado

4½ cups (1080 g) water, plus more as needed

1 cup (200 g) sticky rice

½ cup (100 g) granulated sugar

½ cup (50 g) unsweetened Dutch process cocoa powder

¼ teaspoon kosher salt

1 tablespoon vanilla extract

½ teaspoon instant coffee or espresso powder

Sour Cherry Sauce and Garnish

One 24 oz. (680 g) jar pitted sour cherries

1 tablespoon (8 g) cornstarch

1 tablespoon (12 g) granulated sugar

⅛ teaspoon kosher salt

Whipped cream, for garnish

Toasted unsweetened coconut flakes, for garnish

For the champorado: In a large saucepan, bring the water to a boil over high heat. Stir in the rice, sugar, cocoa powder, and salt and bring back to a boil. Reduce to a simmer and cook over medium-low heat, scraping the bottom of the pot and stirring regularly, until the rice is tender and the mixture is thick like porridge, about 25 minutes (add more water if it gets too dry). Stir in the vanilla and instant coffee. Remove from the heat. Cover and keep warm.

For the sour cherry sauce: Drain the jar of cherries well, reserving the juice.

In a small saucepan, whisk together ¼ cup (60 g) of the reserved cherry juice, the cornstarch, sugar, and salt. Cook over high heat, whisking constantly, until thick (like canned cherry pie filling), 30 to 60 seconds. Remove from the heat and stir in the drained cherries. If it looks too thick, add another tablespoon (15 g) or so of the reserved cherry juice.

To serve, spoon the warm champorado into small dessert bowls. Top with the whipped cream first. Top with the sour cherry sauce and sprinkle with toasted coconut flakes.

Note: Champorado will thicken even more as it cools. If, after reheating leftovers, the champorado is too thick, simply add a splash of boiling water to thin it out. ●

Southeast Tiramisu

My version of tiramisu is padded with thick coconut cream, whipped into a luscious mixture as light and airy as silk gauze. Fresh pandan leaves, known as "vanilla of the East," steps in for Marsala wine, imparting a sweet, grassy flavor and a pale green tint. I'm charmed, as always, by the combination of coconut and pandan. And I steal a few spoonfuls of the pudding for myself before layering the rest with panels of crisp ladyfingers, stained with coffee as dark as ink. This is the part I look forward to the most in tiramisu, the rich roasted flavor of coffee. I prefer robusta beans, which are cultivated in many parts of Southeast Asia, including Indonesia, Laos, the Philippines, and most notably Vietnam.

Compared to other bean varieties, robusta beans are nutty and chocolatey with a bold coffee flavor and a lot of (literally, the most) caffeine. I opt for instant coffee, since it's regularly made with robusta. Growing up, we always kept instant in the house because my mom, like many Filipinos, prefers it to fresh brewed. I highly recommend decaf for this recipe, lest you want to stay up all night. Taste aside, I love how visual this tiramisu is when you cut into it. The pronounced layers and stark muted colors, green and black, are dramatic, stimulating, and delightedly haunting.

In a small food processor, add the pandan leaves and water and puree. Scrape down the sides as needed and resist the urge to add more water. It won't look like it's blending well but you just want to get the pandan really pulverized.

Place a fine-mesh sieve over a small bowl and strain the mixture, pressing with a rubber spatula to extract the green liquid. You should have 3 tablespoons (45 g) of pandan juice (if you're short for whatever reason, just add a little water). Set aside.

In a wide shallow bowl, add the hot coffee, ¼ cup (50 g) of the granulated sugar, and 2 tablespoons (30 g) of the pandan juice. Whisk until the sugar is dissolved. Set aside and let cool.

Bring a pot of water to a simmer (your stand mixer bowl should be able to sit over the pot without the bottom of the bowl touching the water). Fit the stand mixer with the whisk.

In the stand mixer bowl, add the eggs and the remaining ½ cup (100 g) of the sugar. Set the bowl over the pot of simmering water. Cook, whisking constantly, until an instant-read thermometer registers 160°F (71°C).

Fasten the bowl into the stand mixer and beat on high speed until thick and ribbony, about 8 minutes. Transfer the whipped egg mixture to a medium bowl.

In the stand mixer bowl (no need to clean), add the chilled coconut cream (only the solidified part, not the liquid). Beat for a few seconds, just to break it up a bit. Add the whipped egg mixture, the remaining 1 tablespoon (15 g) of the pandan juice, and the pandan extract (if using). Beat on medium speed until just combined, about 30 seconds. There may be little lumps, but don't worry about it.

MAKES ONE 8-INCH (20 CM) TIRAMISU

7 frozen pandan leaves (about 55 g), cut into small pieces (see Note)

3 tablespoons (45 g) water

1 ½ cups (360 g) strong coffee or espresso, hot (preferably decaf)

¾ cup (150 g) granulated sugar, divided

4 large eggs, at room temperature

Two 13.5 fl. oz. (400 ml) cans coconut cream, refrigerated overnight

⅛ teaspoon pandan paste (optional)

One 7 oz. (198 g) package ladyfingers, such as savoiardi

Unsweetened Dutch process cocoa powder, for garnish

Toasted unsweetened coconut flakes, for garnish

Note: In place of frozen pandan leaves, combine the 3 tablespoons (45 g) water with ¼ teaspoon green pandan paste.

I highly recommend decaf for this recipe, lest you want to stay up all night

Working with one at a time, quickly dip half of the ladyfingers into the coffee (1 full second or 2 rapid seconds per side, depending on your counting speed). Place them in the bottom of an 8-inch (20 cm) square baking dish, arranging into a single layer and breaking to fit as needed. Top with half of the custard mixture (about 335 g) and spread into an even layer. Repeat the layers.

Cover with plastic wrap and refrigerate until set, at least 6 hours, but overnight is best.

Before serving, use a fine-mesh sieve to dust the surface with cocoa powder. Sprinkle with toasted coconut flakes. ●

Raspberry Lychee Jelly Jars

This recipe is a grown-up version of the countless jelly cups I enjoyed as a kid. The bitty ones, shaped like a thimble, that came in a range of rich shades, from frosty to neon, and just as many flavors. This version needs only a handful of ingredients: a can of lychees, a palmful of raspberries, and a single pouch of gelatin. Snippets of fruit float within the gel, setting into an enchanting mosaic similar to the swirl trapped inside a cat's-eye marble. The tart raspberry echoes the floral notes of juicy lychee, and stains the jelly my favorite shade of pink: blush. A downy pillow of cream is the final flourish.

In a small bowl, mash 4 of the raspberries well with a fork (you're aiming for puree consistency). Push through a fine-mesh sieve, using a rubber spatula, into a small bowl and discard the seeds. Cut the remaining 4 raspberries into a small dice. Set aside.

Place a fine-mesh sieve over a 4-cup (1 L) liquid measuring cup and drain the lychees, pressing firmly with a rubber spatula to extract as much syrup as possible. This should break up the lychees pretty nicely (if it doesn't, coarsely chop them). You should have about 1 ⅔ cups (400 g) syrup. Add enough water to make 2 ½ cups (600 g) of liquid total and whisk to combine.

In a small saucepan, whisk together 2 cups (480 g) of the lychee syrup mixture and the sugar. Cook, whisking regularly, over medium heat until the sugar is dissolved and the mixture is steaming, 3 to 5 minutes. Remove from the heat and cover.

In a medium bowl, add the remaining ½ cup (120 g) lychee syrup mixture and sprinkle the gelatin evenly over top. Whisk together and let absorb for 5 minutes.

Add the gelatin to the warm lychee syrup mixture and whisk until dissolved. Whisk in the raspberry puree.

Divide the chopped lychees and raspberries evenly among six 5-ounce (148 ml) jars. Dividing evenly, pour the gelatin mixture into the jars. Cover with lids or plastic wrap and refrigerate until set, at least 4 hours.

Before serving, let the jelly jars sit out at room temperature for 30 minutes to take the chill off. Top with whipped cream. ●

MAKES 6 SERVINGS

8 raspberries, divided

One 20 oz. (565 g) can lychees in syrup

2 tablespoons (25 g) granulated sugar

One ¼ oz. (7 g) envelope unflavored gelatin powder

Water, as needed

Whipped cream, for garnish

Special Equipment

Six 5 oz. (148 ml) jars

The grown-up version of Asain jelly cups

Crema de Fruta Trifle

Full transparency, this recipe has a lot going on. It's relatively easy, but does take time (which you can break up over a couple days if it helps). This dessert is a Christmas specialty, so a little extra effort seems fair, especially when it yields enough to feed a crowd. Crema de fruta, meaning "fruit cream," is made with layers of bouncy sponge cake, creamy custard, and fruit sealed within a layer of glassy gelatin. It's essentially a trifle, which is why I build mine in a pedestal dish. It feels more festive this way. Here, juicy peaches, tangy raspberries, and sweet pineapple are suspended in a crimson sheet of tart jelly. I must stress that the vanilla custard should be spread all the way to the glass so it safeguards the cake underneath from the cherry gelatin, which, in a liquid state, is poured over top. A pile of pearly whipped cream, dotted with cherries, is the crowning ornament.

For the cake: Preheat the oven to 350°F (180°C). Grease a 9 × 13-inch (23 × 33 cm) cake pan with cooking spray and line the bottom with parchment paper.

To the bowl of a stand mixer fitted with the whisk, add the eggs and sugar and beat on medium-high speed until thick, pale, and ribbony, about 5 minutes. Beat in the vanilla and salt. Sift the flour and baking powder over the egg mixture and fold until just combined.

Scrape the batter into the prepared pan and spread into an even layer. Bake until golden and a toothpick inserted into the center of the cake comes out clean, about 20 minutes.

Transfer the pan to a wire rack and let cool for 10 minutes. Invert the cake onto the wire rack, remove the parchment, and let cool completely.

Transfer the cake to a cutting board. Using a serrated knife, slice into 96 cubes, cutting the cake crosswise into 12 rows and then cutting the cake lengthwise into 8 rows. Transfer to a medium bowl and cover with plastic wrap (a resealable plastic bag works, too). Set aside at room temperature.

For the vanilla custard: In a medium bowl, whisk together ½ cup (120 g) of the milk and the cornstarch. Whisk in the egg yolks and set beside the stovetop.

In a large saucepan, whisk together the remaining 3 ½ cups (840 g) of milk, the sugar, and salt. Heat over medium heat until warm and steaming, about 5 minutes. Turn off the heat.

Gradually whisk about half of the warm milk mixture into the yolk mixture. Then whisk the yolk mixture back into the saucepan and cook over high heat, whisking regularly, until bubbles are bursting on the surface and the mixture is thick like pudding, 3 to 5 minutes. (Reduce the heat if it's bubbling out of control).

Remove from the heat and whisk in the vanilla. Transfer the custard to a large bowl. Cover with plastic wrap so it touches the surface of the custard directly (this will prevent a skin from forming). Refrigerate until cool, at least 2 hours.

(Recipe continued on following page).

MAKES ONE 3.5-QUART (3.5-LITER) TRIFLE

Cake

4 large eggs, at room temperature

½ cup (100 g) granulated sugar

1 teaspoon vanilla extract

⅛ teaspoon kosher salt

¾ cup (94 g) all-purpose flour

¾ teaspoon baking powder

Vanilla Custard

4 cups (960 g) whole milk, divided

¼ cup plus 2 tablespoons (49 g) cornstarch

6 large egg yolks, at room temperature

1 cup (200 g) granulated sugar

½ teaspoon kosher salt

1 tablespoon (15 g) vanilla extract

Fruit Jelly and Garnish

One 8 oz. (227 g) can pineapple chunks

2 ¾ cups (660 g) tart cherry juice

One 8 oz. (226 g) package frozen sliced peaches, thawed, drained, and dried

¼ cup (50 g) granulated sugar

1½ tablespoons (14 g) unflavored gelatin powder

3 oz. (85 g) fresh raspberries, cut in half

Whipped cream, for garnish

Maraschino cherries, for garnish

(Crema de Fruta Trifle continued from previous page).

For the fruit jelly: Place a fine-mesh sieve over a 4-cup (1 L) liquid measuring cup. Drain the pineapple, pressing firmly with a rubber spatula to extract as much liquid as possible. Add enough tart cherry juice to make 3 cups (720 g) liquid total.

Line a sheet pan with paper towels. Cut each pineapple chunk into quarters and transfer to the lined pan. Dice the peaches and transfer them to the lined pan (keeping them separated from the pineapples). Dry well with more paper towels.

In a small microwave-safe bowl, whisk together ½ cup (120 g) of the pineapple-cherry juice and the sugar. Microwave in 15-second increments, stirring after each, until the sugar is dissolved.

In a medium microwave-safe bowl, add 1 cup (240 g) of the pineapple-cherry juice and sprinkle the gelatin evenly over the top. Whisk together and let absorb for 5 minutes. Microwave until melted, about 10 seconds.

To the large liquid measuring cup with the remaining plain pineapple-cherry juice, add the sweetened pineapple-cherry juice and the gelatin pineapple-cherry juice. Whisk to combine and scrape any bubbles off the top with a spoon.

To assemble: Add half of the cake cubes to the bottom of a 3.5-quart (3.5 L) trifle dish, arranging to create an even layer with the fewest gaps.

Top with half of the custard (about 2⅓ cups [600 g]) and spread into an even layer so the custard touches the glass sides of the trifle dish, creating a leakproof seal.

Scatter half of the pineapple, half of the peaches, and half of the raspberries over the custard (try to distribute them evenly). Gently pour half of the gelatin mixture (about 1⅔ cups [385 g]) over top and refrigerate until set, about 2 hours.

Refrigerate the remaining custard but leave the remaining gelatin mixture out at room temperature.

When the gelatin is set, repeat the layers using the remaining cake, custard, fruit, and gelatin mixture. Refrigerate until the gelatin has set and the custard has soaked into the cake, at least 4 hours, but overnight is best.

Before serving, top with whipped cream and decorate with maraschino cherries. ●

Ube Coffee Jelly

In 1827, Boston's iconic Durgin-Park restaurant opened its doors. The menu was classically New England, and one of its earliest desserts, carried across the Atlantic from Britain, was coffee gelatin. The American dish has since died a slow and quiet death, but not before it crossed yet another ocean to be resurrected in Japan during the twentieth century, where it lives on. It's a delicious example of how food transcends time.

My version, inspired by all the purple ube lattes I order, nestles blocks of jiggly coffee in a thick and nutty ube coconut cream. A pirouette of sweetened whipped cream is the final touch. It's decadent and flavorful, a bewitching contrast of violet and onyx. I double the strength of the coffee (because I *really* want to taste it), so if you plan to serve this in the evening, it's probably a good idea to reach for decaf.

MAKES 4 SERVINGS

2 tablespoons (30 g) ube halaya

¼ cup (60 g) canned unsweetened coconut milk

1 drop ube paste

2 cups (480 g) decaf coffee brewed at twice the strength, at room temperature, divided

1½ tablespoons (14 g) unflavored gelatin powder

¼ cup (50 g) granulated sugar

Whipped cream, for serving

In a small food processor, add the ube halaya, coconut milk, and ube paste. Puree until smooth. Transfer the ube milk to a small bowl and set aside in the refrigerator.

In a medium bowl, add ½ cup (120 g) of coffee and sprinkle the gelatin evenly over top. Whisk together and let absorb for 5 minutes. Microwave until melted, about 10 seconds.

In a liquid measuring cup, whisk together the remaining 1 ½ cups (360 g) of coffee and the sugar. Microwave in 15-second increments, whisking after each, until the sugar is dissolved. Add the gelatin coffee and whisk to combine.

Pour the coffee mixture into an 8-inch (20 cm) square cake pan. Cover with foil and refrigerate until firm, at least 4 hours and up to overnight. Using a sharp knife, cut the coffee jelly into 64 cubes.

To assemble: Add about 1 ½ tablespoons (20 g) of ube milk to the bottom of each 5-ounce (148 ml) glass. Top with the coffee jelly, dividing evenly, and garnish with whipped cream. ●

Sweetened Banana Graham Pudding

Having grown up in the American South, I'm deeply familiar with banana pudding. This one takes a cue from Mango Float Cheesecake Cups (page 128) and employs graham crackers as the cookie to absorb the creamy pudding. Graham crackers have a more pronounced flavor than the more typical vanilla wafers, nutty and toasted and deep. The pudding isn't smooth and it's not meant to be. Instead, it's milky and effervescent, plush with tiny tapioca bubbles, extending a bouncy chew not unlike boba. What really sets this dish apart are the bananas, which are coated in latik sauce, a sweet and sticky coconut caramel so good I could drink it.

MAKES ONE 8-INCH (20 CM) LAYERED PUDDING

Tapioca Pudding

3½ cups (840 g) water, divided, plus more as needed

2 tablespoons (24 g) small pearl tapioca

2 tablespoons (16 g) cornstarch

2 large egg yolks, at room temperature

One 12 fl. oz. (354 ml) can evaporated milk

⅓ cup (66 g) granulated sugar

¼ teaspoon kosher salt

1 tablespoon (14 g) unsalted butter

1½ teaspoons vanilla extract

Latik-Sweetened Bananas and Assembly

½ cup (120 g) canned unsweetened coconut milk

⅓ cup (66 g) dark brown sugar

¼ teaspoon kosher salt

5 medium-ripe bananas (about 2 lb. / 910 g)

8 to 10 graham crackers, plus some crushed for garnish

For the pudding: In a small saucepan, bring 3 cups (720 g) of the water to a boil over high heat. Stir in the tapioca and bring back to a boil. Cook, stirring occasionally, until tender and translucent, about 20 minutes. Strain the tapioca through a fine-mesh sieve and rinse with cold water. Set aside.

In a medium bowl, whisk together the remaining ½ cup (120 g) of water and the cornstarch. Whisk in the egg yolks and set beside the stovetop.

In a small saucepan, whisk together the evaporated milk, sugar, and salt. Heat over medium heat until warm and steaming, 3 to 4 minutes. Turn off the heat.

Gradually whisk the warm milk mixture into the yolk mixture. Pour it back into the saucepan and cook over medium-high heat, whisking regularly, until bubbles are bursting on the surface and the mixture is thick like pudding, 2 to 3 minutes.

Remove from the heat and whisk in the tapioca, butter, and vanilla. Transfer to a medium bowl and let cool while you prepare the bananas.

For sweetened bananas: In a small saucepan, whisk together the coconut milk, brown sugar, and salt. Bring to a boil over high heat. As soon as it's boiling steadily, reduce to a simmer over medium-low heat. Cook, stirring occasionally and adjusting the heat as needed, until dark and thick and reduced to about ½ cup (130 g), 5 to 6 minutes.

Transfer 2 tablespoons (30 g) of the latik to a pinch bowl. Cover with plastic wrap and set aside in the refrigerator. Add the remaining latik to a medium bowl and set aside while you slice the bananas.

Peel and thinly slice the bananas, adding them to the bowl of latik as you work. Fold to combine.

To assemble: Add 4 or 5 graham crackers, breaking to fit as needed, to the bottom of an 8-inch (20 cm) square baking dish. Top with half of the sweetened bananas (about 335 g) and spread evenly. Top with half the tapioca pudding (about 290 g) and spread evenly. Repeat the layers with the remaining graham crackers, sweetened bananas, and tapioca pudding. Cover with plastic wrap and refrigerate for at least 4 hours, but overnight is best.

Before serving, microwave the reserved latik until pourable, about 15 seconds. Using a spoon, drizzle the warm latik over the pudding and garnish with crushed graham crackers. ●

The Filipino Tradition of Pasalubong

It was a Saturday in September. The sun was out, bright and beckoning. Which meant all of New York was, too. The sound of chatter and laughter seeped occasionally through the bay window, where the not-quite-autumn light poured in through the glass. I slung a canvas tote tightly around my shoulder, smiled at myself in the mirror, and shuffled out the door to the rhythm of my own contentment. I'd been living in Manhattan for only a few months and was headed to North Carolina the following weekend. I was excited to reunite with my family, to share my new life with them. And that was the goal of the day—to find little pieces of New York I could take home.

I returned hours later with individually wrapped black-and-white cookies and fresh sesame bagels (both of which I stashed safely in the freezer, complete with a neon post-it note so I wouldn't forget), coffee beans from Zabar's, chocolates from Jacques Torres, and three "I heart NY" T-shirts from Chinatown (I deserve to be judged for this, but it really is a vibe). As I shopped for these items, visions of my mom and sister played on end in my mind. That's the thing about pasalubong. When I buy souvenirs for myself, memories from my trip are locked away inside each little trinket. But pasalubong, souvenirs that I procure for my family and close friends, carry their memory.

In the simplest terms, pasalubong is a gift given to those welcoming you home from travel. But it's also a tradition. And it symbolizes far more than transferring an item to someone in the spirit of giving. It shows that you were thinking about them during your time away, honors your relationship, and shares a piece of your adventure with them. This celebrated custom is well-known throughout the diaspora and acts as an important medium for expressing fondness and affection.

There's no limit to what counts as pasalubong. But the best kinds are specific to a certain area. Naturally, this quite often happens to be food. Regional delicacies permeate the bright islands of the Philippines, doubling as prized pasalubong. These culinary marvels attract determined tourists, curious wanderers, and long-standing residents. Laguna's buko pie, filled with creamy young coconut and wrapped in flaky pastry, stands uncontested. Camiguin is known for pastel buns stuffed with sweet and sticky yema. And you mustn't leave Bacolod without trying Napoleones, the Filipino equivalent of the French mille-feuille. Because pasalubong is deeply rooted in the culture, as well as local pride, it's not uncommon for businesses selling specialized food items to employ the term "pasalubong" as part of their advertising.

Travel and homecoming are two parts of the pasalubong equation. But the magnitude of these elements varies. Pasalubong can simply be a sugar-coated pastry you picked up for the family on the way home from work or tasty treat tins gifted during the holidays. For overseas foreign workers employed in another country, pasalubong is a meaningful practice. It allows them to stay connected with their loved ones, their home, and their heritage. Workers and immigrants unable to travel might send balikbayan (return home) boxes in their absence, which are packages overflowing with pasalubong. Growing up, my mom would mail a balikbayan box to our relatives in the Philippines once a year. We'd fill a huge cardboard parcel with everything from toothpaste and shampoo to American snacks and toys to name-brand clothes and accessories. It was a way for us to share our good fortune and remind our family abroad that they were in our thoughts even when we couldn't see them in person.

Pasalubong creates a bridge between our new experiences and those we've left behind. These items don't have to be expensive or fancy or homemade (although there are plenty of delicious options within the pages of this book). Because pasalubong isn't about the gift at all. It's about the connection that exists between people who care deeply about each other, the only real reason to give a gift in the first place. ●

Pasalubong creates a bridge between our new experiences and those we've left behind.

05

Breads & Pastries

Mango Coconut Rolls

In my early teens, sleepovers were the pinnacle of weekend fun. It was a sacred time for predicting the future with a game of MASH, trading gel pens, and chatting shorthand on AIM. (I'm a child of the '90s). After deliberately staying up all night, my friends and I would slink groggily into the kitchen where I'd pull a blue tube of cinnamon rolls from the fridge and preheat the oven. The orange kind, bright and tangy, was my favorite, and had there been other fruit-forward options, I surely would have begged for them at the supermarket. My thirteen-year-old self would have loved the tropical version I've included here, which skips the cinnamon in favor of sweet, citrusy mango and nutty coconut flakes. The cream cheese glaze, slick like lemon curd and glowing like a golden orange sunset, floods the plush swirled creases. I prefer using freeze-dried mango, ground into a dust, for a couple of reasons. One, the flavor is ultraconcentrated, packing a punch without adding extra water content. Two, it means you can make this recipe year-round (not just when mangoes are in season), because, trust me, you'll definitely want to.

For the dough and first rise: In a small saucepan, melt the butter over low heat. Whisk in the milk and heat until an instant-read thermometer registers between 110° and 115°F (43° and 46°C).

Remove from the heat. Add the sugar, sprinkle the yeast over top, and whisk to combine. Let sit undisturbed until foamy, about 5 minutes. Whisk in the egg and egg yolk.

Fit a stand mixer with the dough hook. In the stand mixer bowl, whisk together the flour and salt. Add the yeast mixture and stir with a fork until a sticky dough comes together.

Fasten the bowl into the stand mixer and knead on medium speed, scraping down the sides of the bowl halfway through, until the dough is soft, supple, and clings to the hook rather than the sides of the bowl, 7 to 10 minutes. The dough will be smooth, stretchy, and sticky.

Grease a large bowl with cooking spray and scrape the dough into it. Flip the dough over (this greases both sides) and cover tightly with plastic wrap. Let rise in a warm place until puffed and nearly doubled in volume, about 1 hour.

For the filling and second rise: Using a spice grinder, grind the freeze-dried mango into a fine powder.

In a medium bowl, using a hand mixer, beat together the mango powder, butter, granulated sugar, and salt until smooth and spreadable.

Press the dough down with your fist to expel the air and transfer to a lightly floured work surface. Pat the dough, by hand, into an 8 × 16-inch (20 × 40 cm) rectangle with a long side facing you. Using a rolling pin, roll out the dough into a 10 × 20-inch (25 × 50 cm) rectangle. (It helps to focus on rolling the length first. And then the width).

(Recipe continued on following page).

(Recipe continued on following page).

MAKES 16 ROLLS

Dough

4 tablespoons (56 g) unsalted butter

1 cup (240 g) whole milk

¼ cup (50 g) granulated sugar

One ¼ oz. (7 g) envelope active dry yeast

1 large egg, at room temperature

1 large egg yolk, at room temperature

3¼ cups (406 g) all-purpose flour, plus extra for dusting

1 teaspoon kosher salt

Filling

One 1 oz. (28 g) package freeze-dried mango (see Note)

1 stick (113 g) unsalted butter, at room temperature

⅓ cup (66 g) granulated sugar

Pinch of kosher salt

½ cup (25 g) unsweetened shredded coconut, toasted

Glaze and Garnish

One 1 oz. (28 g) package freeze-dried mango (see Note)

4 oz. (113 g) cream cheese

4 tablespoons (56 g) unsalted butter, at room temperature

Pinch of kosher salt

¾ cup (75 g) powdered sugar

4 teaspoons (20 g) fresh lemon juice

2 tablespoons (30 g) boiling water

2 tablespoons (6 g) unsweetened shredded coconut, toasted

Notes: Freeze-dried mango by Great Value or Crispy Fruit yield the best results. If you use a different brand, you may need to add more boiling water to achieve the correct consistency for the glaze.

(Mango Coconut Rolls continued from previous page).

Spread the mango butter over the dough, leaving a 1-inch (2.5 cm) border on every side except the long side closest to you. Top with the shredded coconut. Starting from the long side closest to you, roll the dough away from you into a tight jelly roll.

Lightly grease two 9-inch (23 cm) cake pans with cooking spray. Using a taut piece of dental floss, trim away the uneven ends (about 1 inch/2.5 cm on each side). With a serrated knife, score 16 even portions. Then cut with the dental floss.

Divide the rolls between the two cake pans. Cover loosely with plastic wrap and let rise in a warm place until the rolls are puffy and touching one another, about 1 hour.

Meanwhile, preheat the oven to 350°F (180°C).

Bake until golden and an instant-read thermometer inserted into the center of one of the middle rolls registers 190°F (88°C), about 20 minutes. If the rolls are getting too brown, cover loosely with foil.

Transfer the pans to a wire rack and let cool while you make the glaze.

For the glaze: Using a spice grinder, grind the freeze-dried mango into a fine powder.

In a small saucepan, add the cream cheese and butter and cook over low heat, breaking up the cream cheese with a whisk, until melted and combined, 2 to 3 minutes. (The butter will not completely merge with the cream cheese just yet).

Add the mango powder and salt and cook, whisking, until incorporated, about 30 seconds. (It will still look quite separated).

Add the powdered sugar, lemon juice, and boiling water. Cook, whisking, until glazy and uniformly combined, about 30 seconds.

Pour the warm glaze over the baked rolls and sprinkle with the toasted coconut.

To bake the next day, hold off on the second rise. Cover the pan tightly with plastic wrap and refrigerate overnight. The next day, adjust the plastic so it covers the rolls loosely. Let sit out at room temperature for 1 hour. Then transfer to a warm place and let rise until puffy and rolls are touching one another, about 1 hour. ●

Tamarind Cream Danishes

The brisk and fruity flavor of tamarind adds new verve to these buttery Danish pastries, in which an ephemeral rush of astringency is eclipsed by creamy sweetness. This taste sequence is reminiscent of a sweet, salty, and sour tamarind candy I often described as "Filipino Warheads" to curious friends as a child, because they hold you in their grip the same way. These pastries swirl just enough tangy tamarind concentrate into the sweet cheesy filling to make them sing with a whispered falsetto.

MAKES 8 PASTRIES

2 tablespoons (25 g) dark brown sugar

1½ tablespoons (22 g) heavy cream

1 tablespoon (14 g) unsalted butter

1 teaspoon (5 g) tamarind concentrate, such as Tamicon

¼ teaspoon kosher salt, divided

¼ teaspoon vanilla extract

One 8 oz. (226 g) package cream cheese, at room temperature

½ cup (50 g) powdered sugar

1 large egg, separated, at room temperature

1 tablespoon (15 g) water

All-purpose flour, for dusting

One 17.3 oz. (490 g) package frozen puff pastry, thawed

Turbinado sugar, for sprinkling

In a small saucepan, add the brown sugar, cream, butter, tamarind concentrate, and ⅛ teaspoon of the salt. Bring to a boil over medium-high heat. Reduce to a simmer over low heat. Cook, stirring constantly, until thick and glazy, about 1 minute (a channel drawn through the bottom of the pan with a spatula should take a few seconds to close).

Remove from the heat and stir in the vanilla. Transfer to a small bowl and set aside to cool. You should have about 3 tablespoons (50 g) of tamarind caramel. It will continue to thicken as it cools.

In a medium bowl, using a hand mixer, beat the cream cheese, powdered sugar, egg yolk, and the remaining ⅛ teaspoon of salt until smooth.

In a small bowl, whisk together the egg white and water (this is for the egg wash).

Line two sheet pans with parchment paper. Lightly flour a work surface and roll out one sheet of puff pastry into a 10-inch (25 cm) square. Cut into 4 equal squares and arrange on one of the lined pans. Repeat with the second sheet of pastry.

Brush the perimeter of each pastry square with the egg wash. Fold in all 4 corners of each square about 1 inch (2.5 cm) and press the point to adhere (it should now be an octagon). Prick the center of the dough all over with a fork.

Divide the cream cheese filling among the pastries, about 3 tablespoons (35 g) each, adding it right into the center. Spread into a flat mound 2½ inches (6.5 cm) wide—it's okay to go over the tips of the 4 folded points.

Add about 1 teaspoon of the tamarind caramel on top of the cream cheese filling. Swirl with a toothpick. (The caramel will be much stiffer at this point, but just swirl it around the best you can. It will melt into the cream cheese as it bakes).

Brush any exposed dough with the egg wash and sprinkle liberally with turbinado sugar. Refrigerate for 20 minutes.

Meanwhile, preheat the oven to 425°F (220°C).

Bake one sheet pan at a time until the pastries are golden brown, 15 to 20 minutes (both the filling and pastry will look very puffed but will settle down as it cools).

Transfer the pan to a wire rack and let cool for 5 minutes. Transfer the pastries to the wire rack and let cool for 10 minutes before serving.

Enjoy slightly warm or at room temperature. Refrigerate in an airtight container. ●

Flaky Pecan Cinnamon Hopia

My Uncle Nanding runs a turo turo, which translates to "point point," on the edge of San Francisco. It's basically a Filipino birthday party buffet turned Whole Foods hot bar, but way more casual: The metal trays are brimming with Filipino favorites, and customers point to the dishes they want. This is where my Aunt Mary retails her buchi (for my version, see page 186). But the top-selling sweet is hopia, which Uncle Nans makes himself. These bean-filled pastries are similar to Chinese mooncakes, but are wrapped in a very flaky pastry that I can only describe as a cross between laminated pie dough and puff pastry (which is as excellent as it sounds). This magic is achieved by the marriage of two doughs, rolled, stacked, and folded to create an infinite number of thin layers. I use a combination of oil and butter for the most tender, flakiest crust. Packaged snugly inside each tasty parcel is a cozy blend of rich and nutty pecans, woody cinnamon, and sweetened red bean paste. These can be enjoyed warm, cold, or in between. But my preference is when they're minutes out of the oven, toasty, creamy, and crisp.

MAKES 12 HOPIA

Cinnamon Pecan Filling

¼ cup plus 2 tablespoons (114 g) canned sweetened red bean paste, such as Morinaga

½ cup (100 g) dark brown sugar

1 tablespoon ground cinnamon

¼ teaspoon fine sea salt

¼ cup plus 2 tablespoons (53 g) pecans, finely chopped

All-purpose flour, for dusting

Oil Dough

1¼ cups (156 g) all-purpose flour

1 tablespoon (12 g) granulated sugar

¼ teaspoon fine sea salt

3 tablespoons (39 g) neutral oil

4 tablespoons (60 g) ice water

Butter Dough

½ cup (62 g) all-purpose flour

4 tablespoons (56 g) cold unsalted butter, cubed

1 large egg beaten with 1 tablespoon water, for egg wash

For the cinnamon pecan filling: In a medium bowl, stir together the red bean paste, brown sugar, cinnamon, and salt. Stir in the pecans.

Line a sheet pan with parchment paper. Using a 1-tablespoon scoop, scoop 12 mounds of filling (about 20 g each) onto the lined pan. Roll into balls (if they're too sticky to handle, dust your hands lightly with flour). Set aside in the refrigerator.

For the oil dough: In a large bowl, whisk together the flour, granulated sugar, and salt. Add the neutral oil and stir with a fork, mashing the oil into the flour until crumbly and combined. Add the water and stir with a fork until a shaggy dough forms. Knead by hand, in the bowl (just a few times), until the dough comes together into a ball. Shape the dough into a flat rectangle and wrap in plastic wrap. Refrigerate for 30 minutes.

For the butter dough: In a small food processor, add the flour and butter and pulse until the mixture looks like large dough crumbles.

Transfer to an unfloured work surface. Gather and shape into a flat rectangle. Wrap in plastic wrap and refrigerate for 15 minutes.

To combine the doughs, on an unfloured work surface, roll out the oil dough into a 9 × 14-inch (23 × 36 cm) rectangle with a long side facing you.

Place the butter dough between two sheets of parchment paper and roll out into an 8 × 10-inch (20 × 25 cm) rectangle. Remove the top layer of parchment paper and, with a long side facing you, place the rectangle down onto the center of the oil dough rectangle. Peel away the parchment.

Using a small offset spatula, spread the butter dough, pulling it away from the center, so it covers the entire oil dough. This will effectively make the oil dough expand its dimensions, but that's okay.

Starting from the long side closest to you, roll the dough away from you into a tight jelly roll. Roll the jelly roll back and forth on the counter until you have a rope 36 inches (91 cm) long. Coil the rope into a round flat spiral (like a snail) and pinch the tail into the dough to seal. Wrap in plastic wrap and refrigerate for 30 minutes.

On an unfloured work surface, roll out the coiled dough into a 9 × 12-inch (23 × 30 cm) rectangle. It helps to focus on rolling the length first, and then the width. Take your time and use a bench scraper to shape the edges into clean straight sides. The dough is very forgiving and you can roll and shape as needed to even the thickness.

Starting from one of the long sides, roll the dough into a tight jelly roll. Roll the jelly roll back and forth on the counter until you have a rope 24 inches (61 cm) long. Flatten the rope by pressing two fingers into the top all the way across. The flattened top should measure about 1 ½ inches (4 cm) wide.

Cut into 12 even portions, creating little bricks of dough. Transfer the dough to a plate and cover with plastic wrap. Refrigerate for 30 minutes.

To assemble: Line a sheet pan with parchment paper. On an unfloured work surface, roll out a portion of dough into a 3 ½-inch (9 cm) square. Flatten a ball of pecan filling into a 1 ½-inch (4 cm) disc and place in the center of the dough. Fold in the 4 corners and pinch the seams to seal, forming an almost-round puck.

Place a 2¼-inch (5.75 cm) round cutter around the dough and use the end of a small rolling pin (or your finger) to gently press the pastry into a perfect round. Place seam-side down on the lined sheet pan.

Repeat with the remaining dough and filling. Freeze for 10 minutes.

Meanwhile, preheat the oven to 400°F (200°C).

Brush the top and sides of the hopia with the egg wash. Bake until golden brown, 18 to 20 minutes, flipping the hopia over for the last 5 minutes.

Transfer the pan to a wire rack and let cool for 5 minutes. Enjoy slightly warm or at room temperature.

Refrigerate or freeze in an airtight container. Thaw frozen portions in the refrigerator overnight. ●

Pan de Coco Sticky Buns

Growing up, our closest Filipino relatives lived in Virginia Beach. I loved when we visited them. Their house had all the best CDs for karaoke, and my older cousin, Mona, would give me all the cool clothes she'd outgrown. But the highlight of every visit was stopping by Angie's Bakery, which sells Filipino breads and pastries, on the way out of town. I never left without pan de coco, a sweet coconut-filled bun, which I'd eat right away in the car on our drive home. To me, the best part was the filling. And that's the inspiration for these gooey sticky buns, where glossy coconut milk caramel sauce, called latik, is lavishly textured with chewy shredded coconut. As the buns bake, they soak up the syrupy glaze, becoming so slick and squishy they nearly melt in your mouth. The surface glimmers in textured brown, looking messy and plain. But this sloppy appearance conveys just how incredible they are. Every swirl in the batch is as good as the coveted center cinnamon roll.

MAKES 16 BUNS

Dough

4 tablespoons (56 g) unsalted butter

1 cup (240 g) whole milk

¼ cup (50 g) granulated sugar

One ¼ oz. (7 g) envelope active dry yeast

1 large egg, at room temperature

1 large egg yolk, at room temperature

3¼ cups (406 g) all-purpose flour, plus extra for dusting

1 teaspoon kosher salt

Coconut Latik Topping

One 13.5 fl. oz. (400 ml) can unsweetened coconut milk

1 cup (200 g) dark brown sugar

¼ teaspoon kosher salt

1 cup (50 g) unsweetened shredded coconut

Filling

4 tablespoons (56 g) unsalted butter, melted

½ cup (100 g) dark brown sugar

¼ cup (12 g) unsweetened shredded coconut

For the dough and first rise: In a small saucepan, melt the butter over low heat. Whisk in the milk and heat until an instant-read thermometer registers between 110° and 115°F (43° and 46°C).

Remove from the heat. Add the sugar, sprinkle the yeast over top, and whisk to combine. Let sit undisturbed until foamy, about 5 minutes. Whisk in the egg and egg yolk.

Fit a stand mixer with the dough hook. In the stand mixer bowl, whisk together the flour and salt. Add the yeast mixture and stir with a fork until a sticky dough comes together.

Fasten the bowl into the stand mixer and knead on medium speed, scraping down the sides of the bowl halfway through, until the dough is soft, supple, and clings to the hook rather than the sides of the bowl, 7 to 10 minutes. The dough will be smooth, stretchy, and sticky.

Grease a large bowl with cooking spray and scrape the dough into it. Flip the dough over (this greases both sides). Cover tightly with plastic wrap. Let rise in a warm place until puffed and nearly doubled in volume, about 1 hour.

For the coconut latik topping: In a large nonstick skillet, whisk together the coconut milk, brown sugar, and salt. Bring to a boil over high heat. Reduce to a slow simmer over medium heat and cook, stirring occasionally and adjusting the heat as needed, until dark and thick and reduced to about 1½ cups (390 g), 8 to 10 minutes.

In a liquid measuring cup, using a fork, stir together the latik and the shredded coconut.

Grease a 9 × 13-inch (23 × 33 cm) cake pan with cooking spray. Scrape the latik into the pan and spread into an even layer. Set aside.

For the filling and second rise: Press the dough down with your fist to expel the air and transfer to a lightly floured work surface.

(Recipe continued on following page).

(Pan de Coco Sticky Buns continued from previous page).

Pat the dough, by hand, into an 8 × 16-inch (20 × 40 cm) rectangle with a long side facing you. Using a rolling pin, roll out the dough into a 10 × 20-inch (25 × 50 cm) rectangle. (It helps to focus on rolling the length first. And then the width).

Brush the melted butter over the dough, leaving a 1-inch (2.5 cm) border on all sides except for the long side closest to you. Top with the brown sugar and spread it around with your fingers. Top with the shredded coconut. Starting from the long side closest to you, roll the dough away from you into a tight jelly roll.

Using a taut piece of dental floss, trim away the uneven ends, about 1 inch (2.5 cm) on each side. With a serrated knife, score 16 even portions, then cut with the dental floss.

Place the rolls in the pan with the latik topping, arranging them in four rows of 4. Cover loosely with plastic wrap. Let rise in a warm place until puffy and touching one another, about 1 hour.

Meanwhile, preheat the oven to 350°F (180°C).

Bake until golden and an instant-read thermometer inserted into the center of one of the middle rolls registers 190°F (88°C), 25 to 30 minutes.

Transfer the pan to a wire rack and let cool for 3 minutes. Run a small offset spatula around the perimeter to loosen any stuck edges. Invert the rolls onto a serving platter (even a cutting board or parchment-lined sheet pan will do). Scrape any topping stuck to the pan onto the rolls and spread around evenly.

Note: To bake the next day, hold off on the second rise. Cover the pan tightly with plastic wrap and refrigerate overnight. The next day, adjust the plastic so it covers the rolls loosely. Let them sit out at room temperature for 1 hour. Then transfer to a warm place and let rise until puffy and touching one another, about 1 hour. ●

The author's Lolo and Lola on their farm in the Philippines

Maple Spam Shakoy

Every morning, when my mom was a child, my Lolo and Lola would pack produce from the farm into large woven baskets, load them onto tricycles—sometimes one, sometimes three, depending on the harvest—and wheel off toward the market in Paniqui, spinning dust into the air. Together they'd sell the day's goods, keeping an eye out for their suki (special repeat customers). The suki system is the foundation of Philippine market culture. It's essentially an unspoken agreement between buyers and sellers, a form of loyalty that generates repeat customers and vendors you can count on. And my grandparents depended on it. On weekends, they would set up their market stall even earlier. Once their bounty sold, my Lola switched from suki seller to suki buyer (the term applies to both parties). Before returning home, she'd pick up pasalubong (gifts) for the kids. Usually something sweet. Usually, shakoy—a twisted yeast doughnut dusted with shimmering sugar.

I make mine with bread flour for an extra downy chew. Each plush braid wears a veil of satiny maple icing and a generous shower of crispy golden sprinkles, courtesy of fried, finely chopped Spam (a tenured staple of my pantry). For me, it's the best alliance of sweet and salty.

For the doughnuts: In a small saucepan, melt the butter over low heat. Whisk in the milk and heat until an instant-read thermometer registers between 110° and 115°F (43° and 46°C).

Remove from the heat. Add the sugar, sprinkle the yeast over top, and whisk to combine. Let sit undisturbed until foamy, about 5 minutes. Whisk in the egg and egg yolk.

Fit a stand mixer with the dough hook. In the stand mixer bowl, whisk together the flour and salt. Add the yeast mixture and stir with a fork until a sticky dough comes together.

Fasten the bowl into the stand mixer and knead on medium speed, scraping down the sides of the bowl a couple times throughout, until the dough is smooth, firm, and no longer sticky, 8 to 10 minutes.

Grease a large bowl with cooking spray. Shape the dough into a ball and place it in the bowl. Flip the dough over (this greases both sides). Cover tightly with plastic wrap. Let rise in a warm place until puffed and nearly doubled in volume, about 1 hour 15 minutes.

Press the dough down with your fist to expel the air and transfer to an unfloured work surface. Divide the dough into 16 equal portions (about 39 g each). Keep the portions loosely covered with plastic wrap while you work.

Line two sheet pans with parchment paper. Working with one portion of dough at a time, roll it back and forth on your work surface until it forms a 15-inch (38 cm) long rope. Bring the two ends together and twist the dough a few times (I find this is easier to do with the dough flat on the work surface, not in the air). Arrange the twists, evenly spaced apart, on the lined sheet pans.

(Recipe continued on following page).

MAKES 16 DOUGHNUTS

Doughnuts

2 tablespoons (28 g) unsalted butter

¾ cup (180 g) whole milk

2 tablespoons (25 g) granulated sugar

One ¼ oz. (7 g) envelope active dry yeast

1 large egg, at room temperature

1 large egg yolk, at room temperature

2¾ cups (344 g) bread flour, plus extra for dusting

1 teaspoon kosher salt

Neutral oil, for deep-frying

Crispy Spam and Maple Glaze

6 oz. (170 g) Spam, finely chopped

4 tablespoons (56 g) unsalted butter

½ cup (150 g) pure maple syrup

1½ cups (150 g) powdered sugar

1 teaspoon maple extract

(Maple Spam Shakoy continued from previous page).

Cover loosely with plastic wrap. Let rise in a warm place until puffed and swollen (they won't be quite doubled in volume), about 30 minutes.

Attach a candy or digital probe thermometer to a heavy pot or Dutch oven and fill with 2 inches (5 cm) of neutral oil. Heat the oil to 375°F (190°C). Set a wire rack inside a foil-lined sheet pan and set beside the stovetop.

Carefully add 3 of the dough twists to the hot oil. Fry until golden brown, 1 to 2 minutes per side. Transfer to the prepared rack. Repeat with the remaining dough twists.

For the crispy Spam: Place a fine-mesh sieve over a medium heatproof bowl and set beside the stovetop. Line a plate with paper towels.

Into a large nonstick skillet, carefully ladle just enough of the oil used for frying the doughnuts to create a thin layer across the entire surface of the pan. Heat over medium-low heat. Add the chopped Spam and spread out into an even layer. Cook, stirring occasionally, until golden and crisp, 12 to 15 minutes. Watch out for splattering and reduce the heat if needed.

Drain the fried Spam in the sieve and then transfer to the paper towels to drain further.

For the maple glaze: In a small saucepan, add the butter and maple syrup and cook over low heat until the butter is melted, 3 to 4 minutes. Remove from the heat and whisk in the powdered sugar and maple extract. Let rest for 5 minutes to allow the glaze to thicken up a bit.

To assemble: Dip the top of a doughnut into the glaze and set it back onto the prepared rack. Sprinkle with crispy Spam. Repeat with the remaining doughnuts, glaze, and Spam. If the glaze gets too thick as you're working, reheat it over low heat to thin it back out.

Store at room temperature in an airtight container for up to 2 days. ●

Lemongrass Vanilla Scones

I use an immersion blender to crush the lemongrass into a fragrant, juicy paste. It's the best way to unleash its oils, bright and floral and cooling. And this method is quick and painless (though you could get a workout in by reaching for a mortar and pestle). Whatever you do, don't overwork the dough. A gentle hand is the key to nailing a light, tender texture. But another little trick of mine is to cover the scones with a tea towel as soon as they're out of the oven. This traps the heat, creating steam, and thus softening its crumb. The tops are crisp and craggy, emphasized by a sprinkling of pearl sugar for a satisfying crunch. These scones fit in the palm of your hand. And that's how I like them. Not too big, not too small.

MAKES 16 SMALL SCONES

Scones

2 stalks lemongrass, trimmed and first one or two woody layers removed (about 50 g)

⅔ cup (160 g) heavy cream, cold, plus extra for brushing

1 large egg

1 tablespoon (15 g) vanilla bean paste

3 cups (375 g) all-purpose flour, plus extra for dusting

¼ cup (50 g) granulated sugar

1 tablespoon (10 g) baking powder

1 teaspoon kosher salt

½ teaspoon baking soda

1½ sticks (170 g) unsalted butter, cubed small and very cold

Pearl or turbinado sugar, for sprinkling

Glaze

1 cup (100 g) powdered sugar

5 teaspoons (25 g) fresh lemon juice

½ teaspoon vanilla extract

Special Equipment

Immersion blender

For the scones: Slice the lemongrass into small rounds and transfer to a 2-cup (500 ml) liquid measuring cup. Using an immersion blender, blend the lemongrass into a chunky paste.

Add the heavy cream, egg, and vanilla bean paste. Stir together with a fork. Cover with plastic wrap and set aside in the refrigerator.

In a large bowl, whisk together the flour, granulated sugar, baking powder, salt, and baking soda. Add the butter and toss to coat. Using your hands, rub the butter into the flour mixture until crumbly and sandy. Freeze for 10 minutes. Pour the lemongrass-cream mixture into the chilled flour mixture and stir with a fork until a craggy dough forms.

Scrape the dough onto a lightly floured work surface. Shape the dough into a large mound (don't knead it). It won't be smooth and there will be cracks. Divide the dough into 2 equal portions. Pat and shape each portion into a disc 1 inch (2.5 cm) thick and about 5½ inches (14 cm) across.

Line a sheet pan with parchment paper. Cut each disc into 8 wedges and place on the lined pan, arranging them in four rows of four (alternating the direction of the points in each row so they fit better). Refrigerate for 15 minutes.

Meanwhile, preheat the oven to 400°F (200°C).

Brush the scones with a little cream and sprinkle with pearl sugar. Bake until golden and puffed, 18 to 20 minutes.

As soon as they come out of the oven, transfer the pan to a wire rack and cover loosely with a tea towel while you make the glaze (this helps them soften a bit).

For the glaze: In a medium bowl, whisk together the powdered sugar, lemon juice, and vanilla.

Spoon a little glaze over each scone. Enjoy immediately or wait until the glaze fully sets. ●

Turon Baklava

When I was in middle school, my social studies class buried a time capsule, each of us penning a forecast to our future selves. I colored a drawing of myself driving a burgundy convertible, wearing black Jackie O sunglasses, and a big pink bubblegum balloon extending from my red lips. Green palm trees floated in the background because I was moving to LA as soon as I turned eighteen. Our next lesson took us to Greece, and one of the homework assignments was to make baklava. I remember dialing up the internet on my home computer and finding a recipe on the Food Network website, foreshadowing a life I hadn't let myself dream of yet. My mom, who baked them with me, has never been one to look up recipes and follow them. That's not her style of cooking. It was new to see my mom trace her finger down a piece of printed paper, checking to see if the steps turned out the way they were described. We were captivated by our joint handiwork. The baklava was sticky, crunchy, and sweet, dense with nuts and sugary syrup. Between crispy, crackling mouthfuls my mom muttered that it reminded her of turon, a fried banana spring roll, which fractures the same way with every bite.

This recipe merges creamy banana slices and salted cashews between flaky butter-soaked layers of golden phyllo. Cut into tidy squares, each crinkled packet conceals a soft, squishy filling, and a quiet reminder that food can bring people together in unconventional ways.

Preheat the oven to 350°F (180°C).

In a medium bowl, stir together the cashews and cinnamon.

Stack the phyllo dough on a cutting board and keep covered with a damp paper towel while you work.

Brush the bottom and sides of a 9 × 13-inch (23 × 33 cm) aluminum cake pan with a coating of melted butter.

Layer 10 sheets of phyllo in the pan, brushing the top of each sheet with butter before adding the next (butter the phyllo in the pan, not on the cutting board). Sprinkle 5 tablespoons of the cashew mixture evenly over the top sheet of phyllo.

Layer 2 sheets of phyllo over the cashew mixture, brushing the top of each sheet with butter before adding the next. Sprinkle 5 tablespoons of the cashew mixture evenly over the top sheet of phyllo.

Repeat this pattern once more, starting with 2 sheets of phyllo and ending with 5 tablespoons of the cashew mixture.

Layer 2 sheets of phyllo over the cashew mixture, brushing the top of each sheet with butter before adding the next.

MAKES 32 PIECES

2 cups (280 g) lightly salted roasted cashews, finely chopped

2 teaspoons ground cinnamon

1 lb. (450 g) frozen phyllo dough (about 34 sheets), thawed

4 sticks (452 g) unsalted butter, melted

2 almost ripe bananas (yellow with a hint of green)

1 cup (200 g) granulated sugar

1 cup (200 g) dark brown sugar

1½ cups (360 g) water

1½ teaspoons vanilla extract

ORDER OF LAYERS

10 sheets phyllo

nuts

2 sheets phyllo

nuts

2 sheets phyllo

nuts

2 sheets phyllo

bananas

2 sheets phyllo

nuts

2 sheets phyllo

nuts

2 sheets phyllo

nuts

10 sheets phyllo

BOTTOM OF PAN

Peel and slice the bananas thinly into rounds about ¼ inch (½ cm) thick. Top the phyllo with the bananas, arranging in a single even layer. I can usually fit 8 or 9 slices across and 6 or 7 slices down (use your judgment). You may have banana slices leftover.

Layer 2 sheets of phyllo over the bananas, brushing the top of each sheet with butter before adding the next. Sprinkle 5 tablespoons of the cashew mixture evenly over the top sheet of phyllo. Repeat this pattern twice more, starting with 2 sheets of phyllo and ending with 5 tablespoons of nuts.

Layer 10 sheets of phyllo over the nuts, brushing the top of each sheet with butter before adding the next.

Using a sharp knife, slice the baklava into 32 pieces (make sure to cut all the way down).

Bake until the phyllo is deeply golden and crisp, 1 hour to 1 hour 10 minutes. Transfer the pan to a wire rack and let cool for 1 hour.

In a medium saucepan, add the granulated sugar, brown sugar, and water and bring to a boil over high heat. Boil, stirring occasionally, until reduced to about 2 cups (475 ml), about 6 minutes. Remove from the heat and whisk in the vanilla.

Gradually pour the hot syrup over the cooled baklava. Let cool completely, about 6 hours.

Store in the refrigerator. Bring to room temperature before serving. ●

Photo on following page.

Coconut Jam and
Chocolate Ensaymada Loaf

Ensaymada, a Filipino brioche, is a popular specialty bread often enjoyed during the holiday season. It's typically coiled into individual buns and topped with butter, sugar, and a shower of soft, shredded cheese. My interpretation bakes as one large, standard loaf and is very reminiscent of babka (one of my most beloved New York bakery items). The dough is lined and braided with coconut jam (known as minatamis na bao and thicker than the coconut caramel sauce called latik), fortified with chocolate, giving it more body and viscosity as it melts and fuses into one sticky spread. It's gooey and nutty and bold. And, once it's baked, generates the most captivating swirls set within layers of fluffy, enriched bread. It's absolutely dreamy.

For the dough: In a small saucepan, heat the milk over low heat until an instant-read thermometer registers between 110° and 115°F (43° and 46°C).

Remove from the heat and whisk in the sugar and yeast. Let sit undisturbed until foamy, about 5 minutes. Add the egg and egg yolk and whisk to combine.

Fit a stand mixer with the dough hook. In the stand mixer bowl, whisk together the flour and salt. Add the yeast mixture and stir with a fork until a sticky dough comes together.

Fasten the bowl into the stand mixer and mix on low speed, until the flour is more uniformly combined, about 1 minute.

Increase the speed to medium. Gradually add the butter, about a tablespoon at a time, letting it incorporate before adding more (it takes about 3 minutes to add all the butter). Continue to beat on medium speed until the dough is soft and stretchy and doesn't leave sticky residue all over your hands, 7 to 10 minutes.

Scrape the dough onto an unfloured work surface. Cup both your hands over it and roll it around in a circular motion against the work surface until it forms a smooth ball (this doesn't have to be perfect).

Grease a large bowl with cooking spray and place the dough in it. Flip the dough over (this greases both sides). Cover tightly with plastic wrap. Let rise in a warm place until puffed and nearly doubled in volume, about 1 hour 30 minutes.

For the chocolate coconut jam: Meanwhile, in a small saucepan, whisk together the coconut milk, brown sugar, and salt. Bring to a boil over high heat. Reduce to a simmer over medium-low heat and cook, stirring occasionally and adjusting the heat as needed, until dark and thick and reduced to slightly less than ½ cup (about 100 ml), 5 to 7 minutes.

In a liquid measuring cup, using a fork, stir together the latik, chocolate, and coconut extract. Refrigerate until thickened and chilled, at least 45 minutes.

To assemble: Grease a 9 × 5-inch (23 × 13 cm) loaf pan with cooking spray and line with parchment paper so there is overhang on both the long sides.

MAKES ONE 9 × 5-INCH (23 × 13 CM) LOAF

Dough

¾ cup (180 g) whole milk

¼ cup (50 g) granulated sugar

One ¼ oz. (7 g) envelope active dry yeast

1 large egg, at room temperature

1 large egg yolk, at room temperature

3 cups (375 g) bread flour, plus extra for dusting

1 teaspoon kosher salt

5 tablespoons (70 g) butter, at room temperature

Chocolate Coconut Jam

½ cup (120 g) canned unsweetened coconut milk

⅓ cup (66 g) dark brown sugar

⅛ teaspoon kosher salt

2 oz. (56 g) dark chocolate (70% cacao), finely chopped

½ teaspoon coconut extract

Press the dough down with your fist to expel the air and transfer to a lightly floured work surface. Pat the dough by hand into a 9 × 12-inch (23 × 30 cm) rectangle with a short side facing you. Using a rolling pin, roll out the dough into a 9 × 22-inch (23 × 56 cm) rectangle. The dough will be very easy to shape and manipulate.

Spread the chocolate coconut jam evenly over the dough, leaving a ½-inch (1.25 cm) border around the perimeter.

Starting from the short side closest to you, roll the dough away from you into a tight jelly roll. Using a sharp knife, cut in half lengthwise to create two ropes. Pinch and seal the two ends of each rope.

Twist the dough ropes together, forming a braid and keeping the cut sides facing up. (If this feels really soft and sloppy, transfer the dough ropes to a parchment-lined sheet pan and freeze for 10 minutes to let it firm up).

Transfer the braid to the prepared loaf pan, squishing together like an accordion and tucking the ends under to fit.

Spray the top of the braid with cooking spray and cover loosely with plastic wrap. Let rise in a warm place until puffed up over the rim about a half an inch, about 45 minutes.

Meanwhile, preheat the oven to 350°F (180°C).

Remove the plastic wrap and place the loaf pan on a sheet pan. Bake until golden brown and an instant-read thermometer inserted into the center of the bread registers 190°F (88°C), 50 minutes to 1 hour. Cover loosely with foil for the last 20 minutes to prevent overbrowning.

Transfer the loaf pan to a wire rack and let cool for 20 minutes. Using the parchment overhang as handles, lift the loaf onto the wire rack. Remove the parchment and let cool completely.

Store at room temperature in an airtight container for up to 5 days. ●

Photo on the following page.

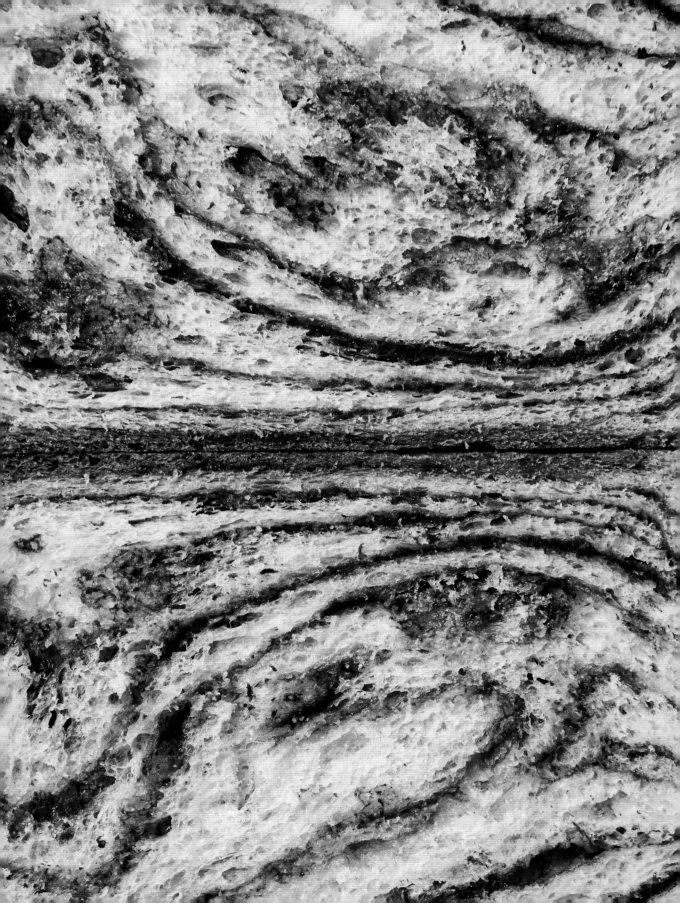

Pandan Napoleones

The city of Bacolod is famous for its pristine beaches, colorful festivals, and architectural attractions. Happiness and laughter are common sights. And because of it, Bacolod is known as the "City of Smiles." Situated within an area known as the "sugar bowl of the Philippines," Bacolod has a reputation for producing some of the nation's tastiest sweets. Many journey far and wide for Napoleones, the Philippine equivalent to the French mille-feuille, which bookends thick, silky custard between two slices of buttery puff pastry. It's extra crunchy, every bite casting crispy flakes all around like a croissant. My version steeps the custard with fresh pandan, a long tropical leaf treasured for its grassy vanilla flavor. The tops are garnished with a blanket of green pandan icing and a gleaming red maraschino cherry right in the center, creating a startling design that looks like it's been inspired by a cartoon (which really makes me smile). I break out my ruler for clean lines and perfectly shaped squares, but don't bother too much if it causes you stress. Napoleones look très chic even when they're rustic.

In a medium bowl, whisk together ½ cup (120 g) of the milk and the cornstarch. Whisk in the egg yolks and set beside the stovetop.

In a small saucepan, whisk together the remaining 1 cup (240 g) of milk, the granulated sugar, and salt. And the pandan knot and heat over medium heat until warm and steaming, about 3 minutes. Turn off the heat.

Gradually whisk the warm milk mixture into the yolk mixture, then pour it back into the saucepan. Cook over medium heat, whisking constantly, until bubbles are bursting on the surface and the mixture is thick like pudding, about 2 minutes.

Transfer the custard to a medium bowl and discard the pandan knot. Cover with plastic wrap so it touches the surface of the custard directly (this will prevent a skin from forming). Refrigerate until fully chilled, at least 2 hours.

On a lightly floured work surface, stack both sheets of puff pastry and cut in half so you have two rectangles. Stack the 4 rectangles and position the stack so a short side is facing you.

Dusting the dough as needed to prevent sticking, roll out the pastry into a 9 × 18-inch (23 × 46 cm) rectangle. (It helps to focus on rolling the length first. And then the width). Trim the dough so you have a neat 8 × 16-inch (20 × 40 cm) rectangle.

Line two sheet pans with parchment paper. Cut the dough in half crosswise so you have two 8-inch (20 cm) squares. Cut each square into 9 squares. Transfer the pastry squares to the lined pans. Freeze for 15 minutes.

Meanwhile, preheat the oven to 400°F (200°C).

Bake one pan at a time until the pastry is golden and puffed, about 20 minutes. Transfer the pan to a wire rack and let cool for 10 minutes.

Meanwhile, line a plate with paper towels. Slice the cherries in half and place them cut-side down on the paper towels. Dry them well (so they don't bleed into the icing) and set aside.

MAKES 18 PASTRIES

1½ cups (360 g) whole milk, divided

3 tablespoons (24 g) corn-starch

3 large egg yolks, at room temperature

¼ cup plus 2 tablespoons (75 g) granulated sugar

¼ teaspoon kosher salt

1 frozen pandan leaf, thawed and tied into a tight knot

All-purpose flour, for dusting

One 17.3 oz. (490 g) package frozen puff pastry, thawed

9 maraschino cherries, stems removed

3 cups (300 g) powdered sugar

3 tablespoons (45 g) water

¼ teaspoon pandan paste

The Philippine equivalent to the French mille-feuille

Using a serrated knife, slice each pastry into two layers (like you're making two pieces of sandwich bread). Place the tops, cut side down, on a wire rack set inside a foil-lined sheet pan.

In a medium bowl, whisk together the powdered sugar and water. It should drip thickly and slowly off the whisk. If needed, add water ¼ teaspoon at a time, until you reach the correct consistency. Whisk in the pandan paste. Transfer to a piping bag and snip off the tip (you can always cut more off).

Working with a few at a time, pipe a layer of the icing onto the pastry tops. I like to pipe a flat even squiggle all over and let gravity settle it into a smooth even layer. Press a maraschino cherry half, cut side down, into the center of the icing. Let them set completely.

Spread 1 heaping tablespoon (about 25 g) of the custard onto the bottoms of the pastries. Sandwich with an iced top. ●

Marbled Ube Banana Bread

When the pandemic officially began, I took refuge at my childhood home in the Southern Outer Banks of North Carolina. In a matter of weeks, banana bread was in the midst of a resurgence. Everyone was baking it and everyone was talking about it. Cooking has long been my form of coping with uncertain times and I remember opening my mom's fridge to grab milk and eggs when I saw a jar of ube halaya (purple yam jam) hiding behind a repurposed plastic container. I plucked it from the shelf and swirled it into my batter. Slicing into the baked loaf revealed marbled streaks of purple. It was tender and creamy, the mellow honeyed flavor of banana merging with the sweet earthy flavor of ube. My husband, Miles, and my mom joined in a chorus of praise. I was happy with it, too. Later that night, when I couldn't sleep, I found myself ruminating about the bread I'd made that afternoon. This is the recipe that sparked the idea for this book—reinterpretations of Filipino American desserts and flavors, and the beginning of my personal renaissance.

MAKES ONE 9 × 5-INCH (23 × 13 CM) LOAF

2 cups (250 g) all-purpose flour

2 teaspoons baking powder

½ teaspoon baking soda

1 teaspoon kosher salt

1 stick (113 g) unsalted butter, at room temperature

¾ cup (150 g) granulated sugar

2 large eggs, at room temperature

3 very ripe bananas, mashed (about 1½ cups/ 360 g)

¾ cup (190 g) ube halaya

¼ cup (60 g) whole milk

1½ teaspoons ube paste

Preheat the oven to 350°F (180°C). Grease a 9 × 5-inch (23 × 13 cm) loaf pan with cooking spray and line with parchment paper so there is overhang on both the long sides.

In a medium bowl, whisk together the flour, baking powder, baking soda, and salt.

In the bowl of a stand mixer fitted with the paddle, beat the butter and sugar on medium speed until light and fluffy, about 4 minutes. Beat in the eggs one at a time. Beat in the mashed bananas.

Add the flour mixture in two additions, beating on low speed until mostly combined but not quite. Finish mixing with a rubber spatula.

In a medium bowl, whisk together the ube halaya, milk, and ube paste until smooth. Add 1½ cups (360 g) of the banana batter and fold until just combined.

In alternating dollops, add the two batters to the prepared pan (I usually do about 3 tablespoons per dollop). Using a butter knife, swirl the batter to create a marbled pattern. Tap the pan firmly against the counter a few times to level out the batter and release any air bubbles.

Transfer the loaf pan onto a sheet pan and bake until golden and a long skewer inserted into the center of the cake comes out clean, 1 hour 25 minutes to 1 hour 35 minutes. (If you see a few stray crumbs, that's okay. But there shouldn't be any sign of raw batter). Cover loosely with foil for the last 30 minutes to prevent overbrowning.

Transfer the loaf pan to a wire rack and let cool for 20 minutes. Using the parchment overhang as handles, lift the bread onto the wire rack. Discard the parchment and let the bread cool completely. ●

The recipe that sparked the idea for this book!

Chocolate Cream Pastel Buns

Camiguin province is known for its pastels, soft buns filled with a sweetened condensed milk custard called yema. My version takes a slight detour. After the yema is cooked (which you'll notice is thicker and stickier than a pudding), dark chocolate is strewn over the top and stirred until it melts in the residual heat. At this point, it almost looks like brownie batter. Once it's fully chilled, its texture is lifted and lightened with whipped cream, diluting its color to a faded caramel. Many recipes bake the filling inside the buns. But this one is piped after the fact, flooding every empty crevice of the plush, springy buns with silky chocolate cream.

For the dough: In a small saucepan, melt the butter over low heat. Whisk in the milk and heavy cream and heat until an instant-read thermometer registers between 110° and 115°F (43° and 46°C).

Remove from the heat and whisk in the sugar and yeast. Let sit undisturbed until foamy, about 5 minutes. Add the eggs and whisk to combine.

Fit a stand mixer with the dough hook. In the stand mixer bowl, whisk together the flour, milk powder, and salt. Add the yeast mixture and stir with a fork until a sticky dough comes together.

Fasten the bowl into the stand mixer and knead on medium speed, scraping down the sides of the bowl a couple times throughout, until the dough is smooth, firm, and no longer sticky, 8 to 10 minutes.

Grease a large bowl with cooking spray. Shape the dough into a ball and place it into the bowl. Flip the dough over (this greases both sides). Cover tightly with plastic wrap. Let rise in a warm place until puffed and nearly doubled in volume, about 1 hour.

Press the dough down with your fist to expel the air and transfer to an unfloured work surface. Divide the dough into 20 equal portions (about 48 g each). Keep the portions loosely covered with plastic wrap while you work.

Line a sheet pan with parchment paper. Working with one portion of dough at a time, cup your hand over the dough and roll it around in a circular motion against the work surface until it forms a smooth ball. Place the balls on the lined pan, arranging them in five rows of 4 and spacing them 1 inch (2.5 cm) apart.

Cover loosely with plastic wrap. Let rise in a warm place until puffed and expanded in size about 50 percent, 35 to 40 minutes. (Not all the buns may be touching, but the gaps between them should be nearly closed).

Meanwhile, preheat the oven to 400°F (200°C).

Bake until golden and an instant-read thermometer inserted into the center of one of the middle buns registers 190°F (88°C), about 10 minutes. As soon as they come out of the oven, transfer the pan to a wire rack and cover loosely with a tea towel for 10 minutes (this helps them soften a bit). Transfer the buns to the wire rack and let cool completely.

For the chocolate cream yema: In a small saucepan, whisk together the milk and cornstarch. Whisk in the sweetened condensed milk, egg yolks, and salt.

MAKES 20 BUNS

Dough

4 tablespoons (56 g) unsalted butter

¾ cup (180 g) whole milk

½ cup (120 g) heavy cream

2 tablespoons (25 g) granulated sugar

One ¼ oz. (7 g) envelope active dry yeast

2 large eggs, at room temperature

4 cups (500 g) bread flour

¼ cup (20 g) nonfat dry milk powder

1 teaspoon kosher salt

Chocolate Cream Yema

¼ cup (60 g) whole milk

2 teaspoons (5 g) cornstarch

One 14 oz. (396 g) can sweetened condensed milk

4 large egg yolks

¼ teaspoon kosher salt

1¼ oz. (35 g) dark chocolate (70% cacao), finely chopped

⅛ teaspoon instant coffee or espresso powder

½ cup (120 g) heavy cream, cold

Cook over medium-high heat, whisking constantly, until thickened and bubbles are bursting on the surface, 4 to 5 minutes. Reduce the heat if the bubbles are bursting out of control. (I recommend a whisk slim enough to get into the corners of the pot since that's where it will thicken first).

Remove from the heat and add the chocolate and instant coffee. Whisk vigorously for about 30 seconds (this will smooth it out and cool it down a bit). If there are some little lumps, don't worry about it. You should have about 2 cups (500 g).

Transfer the chocolate yema to a large bowl. Cover with plastic wrap so it touches the surface of the yema directly (this will prevent a skin from forming). Refrigerate until chilled, about 1 hour.

In a medium bowl, using a hand mixer, beat the heavy cream on medium -high speed until stiff peaks form, 2 to 3 minutes. Set aside in the refrigerator.

When the yema is fully chilled, fold in the whipped cream in two additions. Transfer the filling to a large pastry bag fitted with a medium round tip (such as Wilton #12).

To assemble: Poke a chopstick into the side of each bun and wiggle it around to create a decent-size hollow for the filling. Pipe the filling into each bun (about 31 g each) and dust with powdered sugar.

If you don't plan on eating all the pastels right away, store the unfilled buns at room temperature in an airtight container. Keep the chocolate cream yema in the refrigerator and fill the buns when you're ready to serve. ●

Nutella Coconut Buchi

Fried sesame balls are abundant across Asia. Speckled with seeds and filled with various sweet pastes, this glutinous rice flour pastry began in China, where it's known as jian dui, and migrated throughout the continent embracing local names and native flavors. In the Philippines, these golden globes are known as buchi.

Every afternoon, my Aunt Mary readies her kitchen counter to make buchi. She rolls nine hundred weekly by hand, flavored with ube halaya (purple yam jam) and sweetened red bean paste, and sells them at two local Pinoy eateries around northern San Francisco. She adds the hot water to the rice flour slowly, giving it time to "drink." And the dough should be soft, smooth, and "stretchy like Play-Doh."

My buchi falls back on a favorite childhood combo, Nutella and coconut, which I'd craft into sandwiches, sliced diagonally into two triangles for school lunches. It's rich and nutty, creamy and tropical. Chocolate-hazelnut spread is much looser than traditional buchi pastes, but an ample amount of shredded coconut dramatically stiffens its texture. Nonetheless, I like to freeze tiny orbs of the filling, firming them even more, before enshrouding them in the supple dough. I roll my buchi in a blend of white and black sesame seeds for a toasty checkered mosaic. Once fried, a crisp exterior gives way to an ultra-chewy center and extra-gooey middle. Where buchi is concerned, "Just one more," is a phrase I can't help repeating. But this recipe is worthy of becoming a broken record.

MAKES 12 BUCHI

3 tablespoons (54 g) Nutella

½ cup (25 g) unsweetened shredded coconut

Boiling water, as needed

½ cup plus 2 tablespoons (150 g) water

⅓ cup plus 2 teaspoons (75 g) granulated sugar

Pinch of kosher salt

1½ cups (187 g) glutinous rice flour

¼ cup (35 g) black and white sesame seeds

Neutral oil, for frying

Line a dinner plate with parchment paper. In a medium bowl, stir together the Nutella and shredded coconut. Scoop 12 balls, 1 teaspoon (about 5 g) each, onto the lined plate. Set aside in the refrigerator.

Bring a kettle of water to a boil and set aside (you may or may not need this).

In a small saucepan, bring the ½ cup plus 2 tablespoons (150 g) water to a boil over high heat. Remove from the heat and stir in the sugar and salt until dissolved. Cool for a few minutes. (I like this to be around 150°F/65°C).

Add the glutinous rice flour and stir with a rubber spatula until a soft dough forms. The dough should feel like Play-Doh. It shouldn't be sticky and it shouldn't crack. (If needed, stir in hot water from the kettle, a tablespoon at a time, until you reach the correct consistency).

Fill a mug with hot water from the kettle and set it by your workstation. Divide the dough into 12 equal portions (about 31 g each) and roll into balls. Place them on a plate and keep loosely covered with plastic wrap while you work.

Flatten a ball into a 2-inch (5cm) round. If you see little cracks, dip a pastry brush in the hot water (I use my thumb if it's not too hot) and paint a little onto the front and back of the flattened dough to smooth it out.

Add a chilled portion of the Nutella filling to the center and seal well. Roll the ball between your hands so it's as smooth as possible. Roll to coat fully in the sesame seeds. Repeat with the remaining dough portions, filling, and sesame seeds.

Attach a candy or digital probe thermometer to a heavy pot or Dutch oven and fill with 2 inches (5cm) of neutral oil. Heat the oil to 350°F (180°C). Set a wire rack inside a foil-lined sheet pan and set beside the stovetop.

Using a spider skimmer, carefully lower 4 buchi balls into the hot oil. Fry, stirring occasionally to encourage even browning. After about 5 minutes, the buchi will float to the top. Once they're floating, fry until golden brown, another minute or two. Transfer to the prepared rack. Repeat with the remaining buchi.

Let the buchi cool for a few minutes before serving. Refrigerate in an air-tight container for up to 5 days. ●

Ube Cheese Pandesal

I wrote about pandesal for *The Washington Post* a few years back. It was my first recipe to be published in print, a classic take on the Philippines' most beloved crumb-dusted bread roll. It's a bakery staple, a standard breakfast item, and a go-to choice for afternoon merienda, or snack. *Pandesal* translates to "salt bread" in Spanish but it doesn't taste salty. Instead, it's the ideal canvas for smearing with myriad spreads and plunging into steaming cups of warm beverages. It's as ubiquitous as bagels in New York or baguettes in France. It's iconic. A national treasure.

Late 2019 saw the dawn of a new era for pandesal. The introduction of captivating colors and unconventional flavors were designed by the creative minds of many sheltering in place. Flavored pandesal didn't dethrone the original, but it didn't wither away either. Many bakeries, in the Philippines and Stateside, continue to offer a rainbow of options.

If this new generation has a classic pandesal to crown, it's ube cheese, a regal display of amethyst and gold. Each purple pillow is soft and springy, oozing with melty cheese and creamy ube halaya (purple yam jam). Philippine desserts are no stranger to the company of cheese. Here, its velvety saltiness balances the sweet, vanilla flavor of the nation's most loved tuber. Graham cracker crumbs are scattered over top, adding a toasty crunch and the gentle taste of honey.

What I love about this dish is that it reminds us how food can tell the story of history, and not just our personal ones. It's a marker for critical events, like the pandemic in this case. And how, in the bleakest times, you can find comfort and community in making something familiar, something new.

For the dough: In a small saucepan, melt the butter over low heat. Whisk in the milk and heat until an instant-read thermometer registers between 110° and 115°F (43° and 46°C).

Remove from the heat. Add 2 tablespoons (25 g) of the sugar, sprinkle the yeast over top, and whisk to combine. Let sit undisturbed until foamy, about 5 minutes. Whisk in the ube halaya, the egg, the remaining ⅓ cup (66 g) of sugar, and the ube paste.

Fit a stand mixer with the dough hook. In the stand mixer bowl, whisk together the flour and salt. Add the yeast mixture and stir with a fork until a sticky dough comes together.

Fasten the bowl into the stand mixer and knead on medium speed, scraping down the sides of the bowl halfway through, until the dough is smooth, stretchy, and no longer sticky, 7 to 10 minutes.

Grease a large bowl with cooking spray. Shape the dough into a ball and place it into the bowl. Flip the dough over (this greases both sides). Cover tightly with plastic wrap. Let rise in a warm place until puffed and nearly doubled in volume, about 2 hours.

MAKES 20 ROLLS

Dough

4 tablespoons (56 g) unsalted butter

1 cup (240 g) whole milk

⅓ cup (66 g) plus 2 tablespoons (25 g) granulated sugar, divided

One ¼ oz. (7 g) envelope active dry yeast

⅓ cup (83 g) ube halaya, at room temperature

1 large egg, at room temperature

1 teaspoon ube paste

3¾ cups (468 g) all-purpose flour

1½ teaspoons kosher salt

Filling

¾ cup plus 1 tablespoon (200 g) ube halaya, cold

Twenty 5 g-pieces Velveeta cheese, shaped into 1-inch (2.5 cm) coins (see Note)

¼ cup (25 g) finely crushed cracker crumbs

Note: To portion the 5 g pieces of Velveeta cheese, cut half of a 16 oz. (450 g) block into 24 even squares (you'll only use 20 pieces).

A new generation of pandesal

To assemble: Press the dough down with your fist to expel the air and transfer to an unfloured work surface. Divide the dough into 20 equal portions (about 48 g each). Keep the portions loosely covered with plastic wrap while you work.

Line a sheet pan with parchment paper. Working with one portion of dough at a time, cup your hand over the dough and roll it around in a circular motion against the work surface until it forms a smooth ball. Using your hand, flatten the ball into a 2 ½-inch (6.5 cm) round. Add 2 teaspoons (10 g) of ube halaya to the center of the dough and press a cheese coin into it. Bring up the edges of the dough, and pinch to seal. Dip the top of the bun into the graham cracker crumbs and place seam-side down on the lined pan, arranging the buns in five rows of 4, spacing them 1 inch (2.5 cm) apart.

Cover loosely with plastic wrap. Let rise in a warm place until puffed and expanded in size about 50 percent, about 1 hour. (The buns will not be touching, but the gaps between them should be almost closed).

Meanwhile, preheat the oven to 350°F (180°C).

Bake until puffed, the buns are touching, and an instant-read thermometer inserted into the side of one of the middle buns registers 190°F (88°C), about 20 minutes.

As soon as they come out of the oven, transfer the pan to a wire rack and cover loosely with a tea towel for 10 minutes (this helps them soften a bit). The filling can be quite hot so just be mindful.

Store in a resealable plastic bag in the refrigerator or freezer. Reheat in the microwave. ●

Photo on the following page.

06

Frozen Sweets

No-Churn Halo Halo Ice Cream

For me, there isn't a more nostalgic Filipino dessert than the shaved ice sundae known as halo halo. The name translates to "mix mix" and everyone's mix can be a little bit different. My mom and sister have always liked their halo halo extra milky (like so milky, it basically melts into a drink). I, on the other hand, have always been more particular with my ratios, adding more ice and more toppings along the way, balancing every bite.

Here, I've transformed the classic treat into a no-churn ice cream flavored with ube. In addition to its earthy flavor, the ube tints the ice cream a fairytale shade of purple, which is then bejeweled with red mung beans, multicolor fruits and jellies, and maraschino cherries (which I've been adding to halo halo ever since I was a kid).

I love this recipe because it lets me have halo halo at the ready, stocked in my freezer, waiting for me to sneak a few bites or scoop onto a crunchy cone. Sometimes I even pile it into a bowl with a snowbank of shaved ice for a quick version of the halo halo of my youth. With no shortage of toppings to choose from, every spoonful sends you on a new, wild adventure.

MAKES ABOUT 5 CUPS

¼ cup (72 g) green sugar palm fruit, cut into quarters

¼ cup (70 g) jarred macapuno

¼ cup (68 g) maraschino cherries, cut into quarters

¼ cup (66 g) jarred red mung beans in syrup

¼ cup (62 g) nata de coco, cut into quarters

¼ cup (56 g) canned or jarred jackfruit, sliced

2 cups (480 g) heavy cream, cold

¼ teaspoon ube paste

⅛ teaspoon kosher salt

¼ cup (80 g) sweetened condensed milk

¼ cup (62 g) ube halaya

Line a sheet pan with paper towels. In a colander, add the sugar palm fruit, macapuno, cherries, red mung beans, nata de coco, and jackfruit. Rinse and drain well. Scatter the mix-ins over the lined pan. Pat dry with more paper towels.

In a large bowl, using a hand mixer, beat the heavy cream, ube paste, and salt on medium-high speed until stiff peaks form, 2 to 3 minutes.

In another large bowl, using the mixer, beat together the sweetened condensed milk and ube halaya until smooth and combined. Fold in the whipped cream in three additions. Fold in the mix-ins.

Scrape the ice cream mixture into a 9 × 5-inch (23 × 13 cm) metal loaf pan and cover with plastic wrap. Freeze until firm, at least 6 hours. ●

Malted Banana Split
Ice Scramble

Ice scramble (iskrambol) is a colorful shaved ice slushie typically made with banana extract, powdered milk, and strawberry and chocolate syrups. I blitz two separate mixtures for my version, which relies on fresh fruit. One with frozen bananas and another with frozen strawberries. Both are seasoned with malted milk powder, for an extra dose of richness, and a drizzle of agave to enhance the natural sugars. Stacked with lines of chocolate syrup that fade into the dual-toned layers, each glass is reminiscent of a banana split.

For the banana slushie: In a blender, add the bananas, coconut milk, ice, malted milk powder, and agave. Blend until smooth. Transfer the mixture to a liquid measuring cup and set aside in the freezer. Rinse out the blender jar with cold water.

For the strawberry slushie: In the same blender, add the strawberries, coconut milk, ice, agave, and malted milk powder. Blend until smooth.

To assemble the ice scrambles: Divide the banana slushie between two 6-ounce (175 ml) cups. Top with chocolate syrup. Dividing evenly, top with the strawberry slushie. Top with whipped cream and more chocolate syrup. ●

MAKES 2 SERVINGS

banana slushie

½ cup (90 g) frozen banana slices

¼ cup (60 g) refrigerated unsweetened coconut milk (see Note)

½ cup (80 g) ice

1 tablespoon (7 g) malted milk powder

1 teaspoon (6 g) agave

strawberry slushie and assembly

½ cup (90 g) frozen whole strawberries

5 tablespoons (75 g) refrigerated unsweetened coconut milk (see Note)

½ cup (80 g) ice

2 teaspoons (12 g) agave

1½ teaspoons malted milk powder

Chocolate syrup, for garnish

Whipped cream, for garnish

Note: This recipe uses coconut milk sold in the refrigerator section (not shelf-stable or canned version). Almond milk (or regular milk) works well here, too.

Melon Juice Pops

I have more memories sipping cantaloupe juice as a child than I do drinking lemonade. Both are made with water, sugar, and the fruit's natural nectar. But a cold glass of melon has a distinguishing feature—ribbons of sweet and musky peach-colored flesh, a built-in nibble with every swallow. Here, this classic cooling beverage is frozen into juicy pops, where tender threads of melon are suspended in radiant orange ice.

With one hand, hold a melon half over a medium bowl. With your other hand, scrape the flesh with a melon scraper into long strands, letting the juice fall into the bowl with the strands. Repeat with the second melon half.

Place a fine-mesh sieve over a 4-cup (1 L) liquid measuring cup. In two batches, strain the melon strands, pressing gently with a rubber spatula to extract as much of the orange liquid as possible. Add enough water to the melon juice to make 2½ cups (600 g) total. Set the melon strands aside.

In a small saucepan, add the melon juice mixture and sugar and bring to a boil over high heat. As soon as it boils, remove from the heat. Whisk until the sugar is dissolved.

Divide the melon strands evenly among the ice pop molds. Divide the hot melon syrup evenly among the molds, making sure to leave a bit of space at the top. (If you have a little melon syrup leftover, save it for another use, like mixing with a beverage).

Use a chopstick or skewer to move the melon strands around in each ice pop mold. Let the mixture come to room temperature. Then cover with the lid and insert sticks. Freeze until solid, at least 6 hours. ●

MAKES 10 POPS

One 3 lb. (1.4 kg) cantaloupe, halved and seeded

Water, as needed

½ cup plus 2 tablespoons (125 g) granulated sugar

Special Equipment

Melon scraper (see Note)

Ten 3 to 4 oz. (90 to 120 ml) ice pop molds

Note: Wooden handheld coconut graters are cheaper and easier to source than traditional Philippine metal melon scrapers. They're sold online and in Asian supermarkets.

I grew up sipping melon more than lemonade

Papaya Passion Fruit Ice Candy

If you grew up in the '90s, you're probably familiar with the likes of Otter Pops—frozen, fruity, artificially colored ice sealed in clear plastic tubes. I was also fond of Chucyfru, the Japanese equivalent my family would buy at Asian supermarkets. In the Philippines, pops of this nature are called "ice candy" and are one of the many frozen delights the island offers to allay the sticky heat of its tropical climate. Some are milky, some are fruity, some are chocolatey. In my version, the sweet mellow flavor of ripe orange papaya is balanced by the complex tanginess of passion fruit. Papaya tastes very similar to cantaloupe and has a comparable texture as well, which breaks down willfully into a slick, buttery puree. If you wanted to, you could add a splash of coconut milk for a fresh nutty flavor. Or even a drop of heavy cream, for a little richness. But most of the time, I prefer to revel in the fruits' pure and absolute beauty with no interruptions.

In a blender, puree the papaya until smooth.

In a small saucepan, add the sugar and water and cook over medium heat until the sugar is dissolved. (This will not take long and do not let it boil).

Remove from the heat and stir in the salt. Pour the sugar mixture into the food processor and puree until combined.

Cut open the passion fruit and scoop the pulp (including the seeds) into the food processor. Pulse a couple times to combine.

Transfer the mixture to a 2-cup (500 ml) liquid measuring cup. Stir in the coconut milk or heavy cream, if using.

Using a funnel, pour the mixture into an ice pop bag, leaving a bit of space at the top. Seal or tie the bag and repeat with the remaining mixture. ●

MAKES 8 ICE POPS

10 oz. (283 g) diced papaya

2/3 cup (133 g) granulated sugar

1/2 cup (120 g) water

Pinch of kosher salt

1 fresh passion fruit or 25 g frozen passion fruit

1 tablespoon (15 g) canned unsweetened coconut milk or heavy cream (optional)

Special Equipment

Eight 11 × 2 inch (28 × 5 cm) ice pop bags (see Note)

Note: The easiest place to find these ice pop bags is on Amazon. It's okay to use different sizes of ice pop bags or even freeze them in small paper Dixie cups or standard ice pop molds. Just know that you will not yield the same number of pops total.

Queso Ice Cream

Of all the Philippine desserts that employ cheese (there are quite a few), queso ice cream takes first place, for me. It's as common a flavor as vanilla and chocolate in America. And almost every peddler across the island has it on their carte du jour. My formula is rich with sharp cheddar and lush with cream cheese. I advocate for shredding your own cheese, which, without the added preservatives found in pre-shredded packs, will dissolve evenly into the base mixture. You can double the amount if you don't have cheese powder around, but the powder will upgrade the flavor and enhance its color (I splurge on a gourmet brand with natural pigment, but ivory blends deliver the same delicious boost). Queso ice cream is a sensory journey. It tastes warm and sweet, but feels cold and melting. Try sandwiching a scoop between pandesal or adding a generous swirl of gooey ube halaya (purple yam jam). This, right here, is frozen gold.

In a medium bowl, beat the egg yolks with a whisk. Set beside the stovetop.

In a large saucepan, add the milk, cream, and sugar. Heat over medium heat, whisking occasionally, until warm and steaming, 5 to 7 minutes. Turn off the heat.

Gradually whisk the warm milk mixture into the yolks. Pour the mixture back into the saucepan. Cook over medium heat, whisking constantly, until the custard coats the back of a spoon and an instant-read thermometer registers 180°F (82°C), about 3 minutes.

Turn off the heat and add the cream cheese, cheddar cheese, cheese powder, and vanilla. Whisk until melted and combined. Blend with an immersion blender until completely smooth.

Strain the custard through a fine-mesh sieve into a large bowl or 4-cup (1 L) liquid measuring cup. Cover with plastic wrap so it touches the surface of the custard directly (this will prevent a skin from forming). Refrigerate until cold, at least 4 hours and up to overnight.

Churn in an ice cream maker according to the manufacturer's instructions (mine takes about 30 minutes). It should have the consistency of soft serve.

Scrape the ice cream into a 9 × 5-inch (23 × 13 cm) metal loaf pan and cover with plastic wrap. Freeze until firm, at least 3 hours. ●

MAKES ABOUT 6 CUPS (1.4 L)

5 large egg yolks

1½ cups (360 g) whole milk

1⅓ cups (320 g) heavy cream

1 cup (200 g) granulated sugar

4 oz. (113 g) cream cheese, cubed and at room temperature

3 oz. (85 g) extra-sharp cheddar cheese, grated (about 1 cup)

¼ cup (24 g) yellow cheddar cheese powder, such as Anthony's

1 tablespoon vanilla extract

Special Equipment

Immersion blender

2-quart (2 L) ice cream maker

As common as vanilla ice cream in America

Chocolate Pili Nut Ice Drops

Centuries ago, in ancient Ibalon, there lived a princess named Magayon whose beauty was known for many miles around. A chief and warrior named Pagtuga aspired to win the princess's love. But Magayon's heart already belonged to Pangaronon, a warrior from another tribe. And the pair was set to marry. When Pagtuga found out, he blackmailed the princess into marrying him instead. On their wedding day, Pangaronon launched an attack to win back his true love and the two warriors battled to the death. Pangaronon was victorious. But as he reached for Magayon, she was struck down by an arrow. While Pangaronon cradled his princess, he, too, was killed. Magayon's father buried them together, allowing their love to live on in the afterlife. As the years went by, a hill ascended from their grave. And it grew and grew, forming Mount Mayon, the most active volcano in the Philippines.

Nestled next to Sumlang Lake, on the island of Luzon, Mount Mayon stands as a shapely cone. It's a beautiful place, but also a sacred one in Philippine mythology. Legend claims that when the volcano is at peace, Pangaronon and Magayon are embracing. When white clouds collide at its peak, they're kissing. And when the volcano erupts, Pagtuga is causing trouble.

There's something else that is very special about this wondrous, hallowed site. At the base of Mount Mayon a forest of nut-bearing pili trees thrives, nourished by rainwater and ash-infused soil. Pili trees prosper in extremely stressful environments and are native to the Philippines' capricious volcanic regions. The more trauma it endures, by way of eruptions or typhoons, the more precious pili nuts flower from its branches.

Pili nuts are rich, buttery, and decadent. They add a creamy crunch to these "ice drops," the Philippine term for frozen treats on a stick, and complement the dark notes of the hard chocolate coating (commonly known by its stage name, Magic Shell). When I bite into one of these pops, and the case cracks, and I taste the sweet milky ice cream and the tender morsels of pili nuts, I can't help but visualize Luzon's legendary volcano. I think about how I'm eating one of nature's marvels. And how something so magnificent can rise from such destruction. Just like Mount Mayon itself.

MAKES 8 POPS

1½ qt (1.4 L) your favorite ice cream

1¼ cups (262 g) coconut oil, melted and cooled to room temperature

1 cup (100 g) unsweetened Dutch process cocoa powder

¼ cup (75 g) agave

1 cup (140 g) pili nuts, chopped

To a large bowl, add the ice cream and break it up with a spoon. Let sit at room temperature until soft and spreadable, about 10 minutes.

Spray an 8-inch (20 cm) square cake pan with cooking spray (this helps the plastic stick) and line with plastic wrap so there is overhang on two sides. Make sure the plastic fits snugly into the corners and up all sides.

Add the ice cream to the prepared pan and spread into an even layer. Cover with plastic wrap and freeze until solid, at least 6 hours. (Your freezer needs to be very cold, otherwise the ice cream will be too soft and difficult to work with).

Line a sheet pan with parchment paper (or two quarter-sheet pans if your freezer is small). Run a small offset spatula around the perimeter of the pan so the spatula touches the plastic (not the ice cream directly).

Using the plastic overhang as handles, lift the ice cream square onto a cutting board. Cut the square into 8 equal bars.

Using a large offset spatula and working quickly, transfer the bars to the prepared sheet pan(s). Insert a wooden pop stick into a short side of each bar. Freeze until very solid, about 1 hour.

In a large bowl, whisk together the melted coconut oil, cocoa powder, and agave. Transfer the mixture to a drinking glass wide enough to dip the pops into.

Working with one at a time (and keeping the rest in the freezer), dip the pop into the chocolate mixture until fully coated. Allow any excess to drip off and sprinkle both sides with pili nuts. Let the coating harden before returning it to the sheet pan(s) in the freezer. ●

Mais Con Yelo Pop

Inspired by mais con yelo, a corn-infused shaved ice sundae, these pops start out by stirring together buttery creamed corn and sticky sweetened condensed milk. This mixture is thick like pudding, but only for a moment. As soon as the vanilla ice cream is added (coconut would also taste great), the inherent warmth melts everything down, leaving behind a thinner, pourable solution. Frozen onto wooden sticks and wrapped in crispy cornflakes, each mouthful moves from crunchy to creamy to cold.

MAKES 10 POPS

One 14.75 oz. (418 g) can cream-style corn

¼ cup (80 g) sweetened condensed milk

1 pint (473 ml) vanilla ice cream

2½ cups (100 g) cornflakes cereal, crushed

Special Equipment

Ten 3 to 4 oz. (90 to 120 ml) ice pop molds

In a large bowl, stir together the cream-style corn and sweetened condensed milk. Add the vanilla ice cream and stir until combined and the mixture has turned liquidy. Transfer to a large liquid measuring cup.

Divide the mixture evenly among ten 3- to 4-ounce (90 to 120 ml) ice pop molds. Cover with the lids and insert wooden sticks. Freeze until solid, at least 6 hours, but overnight is best.

Unmold the pops and transfer them to a parchment-lined sheet pan. Let sit for 5 minutes until softened slightly.

Add the cornflakes to a shallow bowl. Dip the pops in the cornflakes, pressing the cereal on by hand as needed, until coated. Return the pops to the lined pan and freeze until very solid, about 30 minutes. ●

Black Sesame Ice Buko

Ice buko, or coconut ice pops, are easy to come by throughout the Philippine islands. They're sold in neighborhood convenience shops called sari-saris, buzzing market stalls, and on the streets by way of traveling peddlers called sorbeteros. The meat of buko, or green young coconut, is tender, slippery, and semi-gelatinous—unlike the firm meat of the older brown coconut. Buko, when in pop form, is often paired with starchy sweetened red mung beans. But the fresh and frosty coconut base offers a clean slate for infinite mix-ins. My version is striped with inky ribbons of black sesame paste, forcing dark and nutty to intersect with light and creamy. It's chilly and refreshing, like you're sipping straight from a coconut ice crystal.

Dip the tip of a wooden skewer into the sesame paste and use it paint swoops and stripes onto the insides of ten 3 to 4 oz. (90 ml to 120 ml) ice pop molds. Freeze until solid, about 30 minutes.

In a blender, add the coconut meat, coconut water, heavy cream, and sweetened condensed milk. Puree until smooth.

Divide the mixture evenly among the molds, making sure to leave a bit of space at the top. Cover with the lid and insert wooden sticks. Freeze until solid, at least 6 hours. ●

MAKES 10 POPS

1 tablespoon (15 g) black sesame paste

¾ cup (113 g) coarsely chopped young coconut meat (see Note)

1½ cups (360 g) coconut water

¾ cup (180 g) heavy cream

½ cup (160 g) sweetened condensed milk

Special Equipment

Ten 3 to 4 oz. (90 ml to 120 ml) ice pop molds

Note: You'll need two young coconuts (I prefer the ivory ones with the pointed tops that have already been shaved), 2 to 2½ pounds (910 g to 1.1 kg) each. You can also use frozen young coconut meat, which is sold in Asian supermarkets, but I really do think fresh is a million times better. To make this with dried unsweetened shredded coconut, use 2 cups (100 g).

Brazo de Mercedes Ice Cream Cake

Brazo de Mercedes can be prepared one of two ways: as a fluffy meringue jelly roll or as a frozen multilayered meringue ice cream cake (like this recipe). This is a grand dessert, to be sure. And my version, built in a loaf pan, spares no splendor. Between you and me, its glamour is a little bit of a façade, because this is actually pretty easy to make. Here, a buttery graham cracker crust book-ends sheets of mango sorbet, coconut dragon fruit ice cream, and silky yema, a rich sweetened condensed milk custard. This tropical stack is topped with a mountain of plush and satiny meringue, which is caramelized with a kitchen torch until dusky and bronze and given the slightest hint of smokiness. Each slice is an exhibit of contrasting textures, sharp lines, and vibrant colors. But this isn't all for show. The flavors play off each other, balancing tangy with sweet, nutty with creamy, and finishing it all off with what is essentially a toasted marshmallow.

For the yema: In a small saucepan, whisk together the milk and cornstarch. Whisk in the sweetened condensed milk, egg yolks, and salt. Cook over medium-high heat, whisking constantly, until thickened and bubbles are bursting on the surface, 4 to 5 minutes. Reduce the heat if the bubbles are bursting out of control. (I recommend a whisk slim enough to get into the corners of the pot since that's where it will thicken first).

Remove from the heat and whisk vigorously for about 30 seconds (this will smooth it out and cool it down a bit). If there are some little lumps, don't worry about it. Whisk in the vanilla. You should have almost 2 cups (450 g).

Transfer the yema to a large bowl. Cover with plastic wrap so it touches the surface of the yema directly (this will prevent a skin from forming). Refrigerate until chilled, about 1 hour.

For the ice cream layers: To a large bowl, add the mango sorbet and break it up with a metal spoon. Let it sit out at room temperature, stirring every now and then, until it's soft and spreadable (but not melted), about 10 minutes.

Meanwhile, spray a 9 × 5-inch (23 × 13 cm) metal loaf pan with cooking spray (this helps the plastic stick) and line with plastic wrap so that there is overhang on all sides. Make sure the plastic fits snugly in the corners and up all the sides.

Add a layer of graham crackers to the bottom of the pan, breaking to fit as needed. Dollop the mango sorbet on top of the graham crackers and spread into an even layer. Set aside in the freezer.

In a blender, puree the coconut ice cream and dragon fruit until smooth and creamy. Pour the coconut–dragon fruit mixture evenly over the mango sorbet (the mango sorbet won't be frozen yet and that's totally fine) and spread into an even layer. Continue to freeze until the yema is totally chilled.

Dollop the yema evenly over the coconut–dragon fruit mixture (this makes it easier to spread evenly, especially if the ice cream is still soft). Spread carefully to prevent mixing the layers. At this point the loaf pan will nearly be packed to the brim.

(Recipe continued on following page).

MAKES ONE 9 × 5-INCH (23 × 13 CM) ICE CREAM LOAF CAKE

Yema and Ice Cream Layers

¼ cup (60 g) whole milk

2 teaspoons (5 g) cornstarch

One 14 oz. (397 g) can sweetened condensed milk

4 large egg yolks

¼ teaspoon kosher salt

1 teaspoon vanilla bean paste or extract

1 pint (473 ml) mango sorbet

6 or 7 graham crackers

1 pint (473 ml) coconut ice cream

6 oz. (170 g) frozen red dragon fruit (about 1 cup)

Meringue Topping

3 large egg whites, at room temperature

6 tablespoons (75 g) granulated sugar

¼ teaspoon cream of tartar

Pinch of kosher salt

Special Equipment

Kitchen torch

(Brazo de Mercedes Ice Cream Cake continued from previous page).

Gently press a layer of graham crackers into the yema, breaking to fit as needed. Cover tightly with plastic wrap. Freeze until solid, preferably over-night.

Remove the top layer of plastic wrap from the pan. Fill a baking dish with boiling water and dip the loaf pan in the water for a few seconds. Invert the ice cream cake onto a serving platter (even a quarter-sheet pan will do). Remove the pan and plastic wrap. (Clean any drips along the layers by scraping with a small offset spatula). Set aside in the freezer while you make the meringue.

For the meringue: Bring a pot of water to a simmer (your stand mixer bowl should be able to sit over the pot without the bottom of the bowl touching the water). Fit the stand mixer with the whisk.

In the stand mixer bowl, whisk together the egg whites, sugar, cream of tar-tar, and salt. Set the bowl over the pot of simmering water and cook, whisk-ing constantly, until the sugar is dissolved and an instant-read thermometer registers 160°F (71°C), about 5 minutes.

Fasten the bowl into the stand mixer and beat on high speed until glossy stiff peaks form (peaks should stand straight up and not curl at the tip), 2 to 4 minutes.

To assemble: Dollop the meringue on top of the ice cream cake. Spread, swooping and swirling, to create whimsical peaks. Toast the meringue with a kitchen torch.

Note: The entire dessert can be made ahead of time and stored in the freezer. The meringue, once frozen, will be soft and squishy (not solid). For clean slices, wipe the blade of your knife between cuts. ●

Pocky Panda Cookie Ice Cream

I'll never forget my first big breakup in high school. And not just because it's a rite of passage for many. First off, I wasn't actually allowed to have a boyfriend. Second, immediately after it happened, my now–ex comforted me by comparing my heartbreak to Sheryl Crow's version of "The First Cut Is the Deepest" (which I think is just so Y2K). I remember driving myself home in silence. And later that night, to quell my teenage despair, I ripped open the freezer in search of cookies-and-cream ice cream. I didn't find it, which sent me into melodramatic agony. I snatched a carton of vanilla bean ice cream and crushed a box of strawberry Pocky sticks and a few chocolate Hello Panda cookies into my bowl, along with a few tears (just kidding).

I took this combination with me to college, where it fueled my late-night study sessions and regular sugar cravings. Pocky and Pandas have been my go-to Asian cookies of choice ever since I was little. And they're fantastic with vanilla ice cream. But if there are others you like best, by all means, make this your own.

MAKES ABOUT 3 ½ CUPS (1 L)

1 cup (240 g) heavy cream, cold

5 tablespoons (62 g) granulated sugar

Pinch of kosher salt

½ cup (120 g) whole milk, cold

1 teaspoon vanilla bean paste

Two 1.41 oz. (40 g) boxes strawberry Pocky sticks, crushed

Two 1.45 oz. (41 g) boxes chocolate Hello Panda or Koala's March cookies, crushed

Special Equipment

2-quart (2 L) ice cream maker

To the bowl of a stand mixer fitted with the whisk, add the heavy cream, sugar, and salt. Beat on medium speed until soft but sturdy peaks form, about 2 minutes. Add the milk and vanilla and beat on low speed until combined.

Churn in an ice cream maker according to the manufacturer's instructions (mine takes about 20 minutes). It should look like the consistency of soft serve (but the texture will be more airy). Add the crushed cookies in the last 5 minutes.

Scrape the ice cream in to a 9 × 5-inch (23 × 13 cm) metal loaf pan and cover with plastic wrap. Freeze until firm, at least 4 hours. ●

Guava Coconut Ice Cream

I brought a pint of this ice cream with me on a recent trip to visit my sister in Washington, DC. When I woke up in the morning, I found her in the kitchen, leaning against the counter, eating straight from the container. It was only 8:00 a.m. and I raised my eyebrows in question. She responded, "My house, my mouse," which is a silly catchphrase we've been saying ever since the height of The Sims, a best-selling computer game that dominated the 2000s. In our sibling nomenclature, this translates to, "My house, my rules."

Here, the fruity, flowery sweetness of guava balances the creamy, buttery flavor of coconut. Its texture is thick and downy, and its color like a dark rose quartz. It tastes like a breezy tropical vacation, warming and revitalizing, like you went for a dip in a cold pool and dried off under the glow of the sun. When there's some in the freezer, it is kind of hard to ignore. No matter the time of day.

MAKES ABOUT 4½ CUPS (1 L)

8 oz. (225 g) guava paste, cubed

⅔ cup (160 g) guava concentrate (such as Dafruta) or water

Two 13.5 fl. oz. (400 ml) cans unsweetened coconut milk, divided

½ cup (100 g) granulated sugar

½ cup (25 g) unsweetened shredded coconut, toasted

4 teaspoons (10 g) cornstarch

¼ teaspoon kosher salt

½ teaspoon coconut extract

6 drops pink gel food coloring (optional; see Note)

Special Equipment

Immersion blender

2-quart (2 L) ice cream maker

Note: I use the color Deep Pink by Chefmaster.

In a large saucepan, add the guava paste and guava juice (or water). Cook over medium-low heat, breaking up the paste with a whisk, until the mixture looks like a thick puree, 7 to 10 minutes. (It's okay if there are a few lumps. Don't let it simmer).

Remove from the heat and add the toasted coconut and a splash of the coconut milk. Blend with an immersion blender until as smooth as possible. Add the remaining coconut milk, sugar, cornstarch, and salt. Blend once more.

Return to the stovetop and bring to a boil over high heat. Once it's at a boil, cook, whisking constantly, until darkened in color and thickened enough to coat the back of a spoon, about 1 minute. Remove from the heat and whisk in the coconut extract and food coloring (if using).

Transfer the mixture to a 4-cup (1 L) liquid measuring cup. Cover with plastic wrap so it touches the surface of the custard directly (this will prevent a skin from forming). Refrigerate until cold, at least 4 hours and up to overnight.

Churn in an ice cream maker according to the manufacturer's instructions (mine takes about 30 minutes). It should have the consistency of frozen yogurt. Scrape the ice cream in to a 9 × 5-inch (23 × 13 cm) metal loaf pan and cover with plastic wrap. Freeze until firm, at least 4 hours.

Peach Mango Sticky Rice Ice Cream

I never leave Jollibee, a Filipino fast-food chain as popular as American McDonald's, without a peach mango pie. Its charm is manifested here alongside sticky rice ice cream, which also pays tribute to Thai mango sticky rice. Because the base is made with glutinous rice, the frozen texture is very unlike typical ice cream. And that, for me, is the best part. It's soft, supple, and satisfyingly stretchy. Its sweet starchy flavor, as comforting as rice pudding, is punctuated with bright pops of tangy puree. My mom said this is the best ice cream she's ever had. But she's my mom and she says things like that.

For the sticky rice ice cream: In a large saucepan, whisk together the cornstarch and coconut milk. Whisk in the sugar and salt. Bring to a boil over high heat. Once it's at a boil, cook, whisking constantly, until thick enough to coat the back of a spoon, about 1 minute. Remove from the heat, cover with a lid, and set mixture aside.

In a medium bowl, add the rice and enough water to cover. Swish your hand around in the bowl until the water turns a milky, cloudy white. Strain through a sieve. Repeat three more times until the water runs clear. Drain the rice well.

Transfer the rice to a small saucepan and add ½ cup (120 g) of the rice milk. Bring to a boil over high heat. Reduce to a very gentle simmer over low heat. Cover with a lid and cook until the rice is tender and the liquid is absorbed, 8 to 10 minutes.

Remove from the heat. Add the remaining 6 tablespoons (90 g) of rice milk and a splash of the warm coconut milk mixture. Blend with an immersion blender until as smooth as possible.

Pour the rice mixture into the saucepan with the warm coconut milk mixture. Blend once more.

Transfer the mixture to a 4-cup (1 L) liquid measuring cup. Cover with plastic wrap so it touches the surface of the custard directly (this will prevent a skin from forming). Refrigerate until cold, at least 4 hours.

For the peach mango puree: In a small saucepan, add the mango and peaches. Use a small silicone spatula to dice up the peaches in the saucepan. Add 2 tablespoons (30 g) of the peach syrup, the sugar, and salt. Bring to a simmer over medium-low heat. Cook, stirring occasionally and adjusting the heat as needed, until the fruit is very tender and starting to break down, about 10 minutes.

In a small bowl, whisk together the cornstarch and water. Stir the mixture into the saucepan. Cook over medium-low heat, stirring constantly, until very thick, about 2 minutes (you may not see any bubbles, but you'll feel it thicken). Remove from the heat.

Blend with an immersion blender until smooth. Transfer the puree to a small bowl and let it cool to room temperature. Cover with plastic and refrigerate until chilled, at least 2 hours.

(Recipe continued on following page).

MAKES ABOUT 6 CUPS (1.4 L)

Sticky Rice Ice Cream

4 teaspoons (10 g) cornstarch

Two 13.5 fl. oz. (400 ml) cans unsweetened coconut milk

¾ cup (150 g) granulated sugar

¼ teaspoon kosher salt

½ cup (100 g) sticky rice

½ cup (120 g) plus 6 tablespoons (90 g) rice milk, divided

Peach Mango Puree

7 oz. (100 g) diced yellow Ataulfo mango (about ½ cup)

One 8.5 oz. (241 g) can sliced peaches, drained and syrup reserved

3 tablespoons (36 g) granulated sugar

⅛ teaspoon kosher salt

1 tablespoon (8 g) cornstarch

1 tablespoon (15 g) water

Special Equipment

Immersion blender

2-quart (2 L) ice cream maker

(Peach Mango Sticky Rice Ice Cream continued from previous page).

To assemble: Churn the sticky rice mixture (it will be thick) in an ice cream maker according to the manufacturer's instructions (mine takes about 20 minutes). It should have the consistency of soft serve.

Scrape half of the ice cream (about 445 g) into a 9 × 5-inch (23 × 13 cm) metal loaf pan. Dollop with half of the peach-mango puree and swirl with a butter knife. Repeat with the remaining ice cream and peach-mango puree. (Don't overdo the swirling or you won't get a nice contrast). Cover with plastic wrap and freeze until firm, at least 4 hours. ●

Soursop Sorbet

My first summer job was at thirteen selling shrimp at a roadside stand in the Southern Outer Banks. It was a simple setup. There was a row of blue and red coolers, packed with ice and shrimp sorted by size, one large metal scale for weighing, and a basket of plastic shopping bags from the grocery store down the street. Some days the owner would stop by with plastic cups of Italian ice (which really had the smooth texture of sorbet) to help us cool off from the afternoon sun. They'd be melted by the time he got there, but we'd toss them in a cooler of shrimp for 10 minutes and let them firm back up again. I'd savor every bite of that frost.

Tropical soursop is a beautiful choice for frozen treats. It's tart and bright, with a flavor that combines pineapple, strawberry, and banana in one. You can gather its ambrosial nectar by pureeing and straining it fresh or melting down store-bought frozen pulp. Both will work. This sorbet is crisp and invigorating, churned until it transforms into velvet snow. In the midst of summer, when the sky burns with heat and the air is soggy with humidity, nothing delivers more relief than tangy, icy sweetness.

MAKES ABOUT 4 CUPS

¾ cup (180 g) water

¾ cup (150 g) granulated sugar

16 oz. (454 g) fresh soursop or frozen pulp

Special Equipment

2-quart (2 L) ice cream maker

To a small saucepan, add the water and sugar and bring to a boil over medium-high heat. Reduce to a simmer over medium-low heat. Cook, whisking occasionally, until the sugar is dissolved and the mixture is slightly syrupy, 3 to 5 minutes. Transfer the syrup to a medium bowl or liquid measuring cup and refrigerate until cold, at least 1 hour.

In a blender, add the soursop and chilled syrup and puree until smooth. Strain the mixture through a fine-mesh sieve.

Churn in an ice cream maker according to the manufacturer's directions (mine takes about 20 minutes). Scrape the sorbet into a 9 × 5-inch (23 × 13 cm) metal loaf pan and cover with plastic wrap. Freeze until firm, at least 3 hours. ●

Acknowledgments

Writing this book has been one of the most challenging, rewarding things I've ever done, and I'm incredibly grateful for this opportunity. It's because of the hard work, confidence, and friendship of so many people that this book is here, a real tangible thing in your hands.

A million thanks to my amazing literary agent, Sharon Bowers. Thank you for your constant encouragement, endless wit, and for believing in me from the start.

I'm especially grateful to my editor, Jenny Wapner at Hardie Grant, who dedicated her time and expertise and graciously shepherded me through my first book. Thank you for putting your faith in me and believing in this project. I'm also indebted to Carolyn Insley and Kate Slate for the careful edits and input.

A heartfelt thank you to my amazing photographer, Linda Xiao, who, with her incredible talent and poise, brought depth and energy to every image. I'm so appreciative of you and Christina Zhang for your attention to detail. Many thanks to my friend and stylist, Molly Wenk, who made every recipe look more beautiful than I ever could. To Tara Holland, I'm grateful for your endless assistance and positivity in the kitchen (and for the daily cups of English tea). Thank you to Maeve Sheridan, for supplying such charming props, and to Ashleigh Sarbone, who went above and beyond with prop styling. It was such a privilege to work with each of you.

My appreciation also goes to Amanda Jane Jones, who skillfully designed the pages of this book. I can't thank you enough for bringing so much color and joy to this project.

I'd like to thank everyone at the Food Network culinary department. You accepted me, inspired me, and gave me a home away from home. Cooking beside you has been one of my greatest joys. A special thank you to Ginevra Iverson, who gave me my first real

shot and took me under her wing. I wouldn't be where I am without you.

To every editor I've worked with, thank you for giving me the space to share my stories. For your steady guidance and confidence. You've helped make me a better, more thoughtful writer. And it means more to me than you know.

To Mom, your sacrifices have given me a better life and I'm grateful for it. Thank you for always making me feel like my cooking is the single best thing ever. Thanks also to my extended family for passing down recipes and stories and continually cheering me on.

Last but not least, to Miles, thank you for being my #1 taste tester, my sounding board, and my biggest fan. From urgent grocery runs to reading early drafts of my manuscript, you've supported me through this process in so many ways. I love you. ●

Index

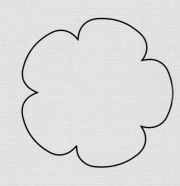

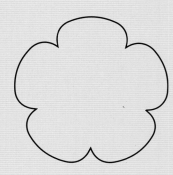

About the Author

Arlyn Osborne is a freelance food writer and recipe developer. After graduating from The French Culinary Institute in New York City, she joined the editorial team at *Food & Wine* magazine before landing at Food Network. While there, she worked in culinary production and food styling before becoming a recipe developer and regular host on the Food Network Kitchen streaming platform. Her work has since been featured in *Bon Appétit*, *The Washington Post*, Food52, and Serious Eats. She lives with her husband, Miles, and their two pups, Winnie and Pip. Originally from the Southern Outer Banks, she currently splits her time between Raleigh, North Carolina, and New York City.